DATE DUE

AUG 3 0 2001		
SEP 2 0 2001		
OCT 2 8 2001		
		EIVED

Demco, Inc. 38-293

808
Writes

JUL 0 0 2001

WRITERS
ON
WRITING

Writers
on Writing

COLLECTED ESSAYS FROM
The New York Times

INTRODUCTION BY

John Darnton

TIMES BOOKS
Henry Holt and Company   New York

Times Books
Henry Holt and Company, LLC
Publishers since 1866
115 West 18th Street
New York, New York 10011

Library of Congress Cataloging-in-Publication Data

Writers on writing : collected essays from The New York times ;
introduction by John Darnton.—1st ed.
p.   cm.
ISBN 0-8050-6741-8
1. Authorship.   I. New York times.

PN137 .W734 2001
808'.02—dc21   00-053509

First Edition 2001

Designed by Paula Russell Szafranski

Printed in the United States of America

1   3   5   7   9   10   8   6   4   2

CONTENTS

DAMAGE NOTED

Contents

INTRODUCTION

John Darnton

I got the idea for the *Writers on Writing* series shortly after I decided to become—of all things—a writer. Actually, to be a stickler about it, I didn't really *decide* to become a writer. As with many of life's intriguing surprises, the decision sort of crept up on me and made itself.

I had been thirty years in the newspaper business (where I still am). Much of that time had been spent abroad, covering Africa, Europe (East and West) and the Middle East. During that time I tried to craft my stories in what I thought of as a writerly way, with plenty of what the foreign desk would call "color." But despite the fact that I sent hundreds of thousands of words halfway around the world by every conceivable means, and despite the fact that those words were presented in configurations called *stories*, I didn't conceive of myself as a *writer*. Like most foreign correspondents, I prided myself on getting the facts in a difficult situation, not on how those facts were arranged. Nor did I object when we called ourselves "hacks," the self-denigrating term of preference, though in our heart of hearts when we said it, we didn't believe it. (If you ever want to reach a reporter with a compliment, don't tell him that he dug out all the facts or presented them fairly; tell him he writes brilliantly and then you'll see his chest swell.) Once I was invited to a writers' workshop in Vermont and I experienced deep ambivalence: I was pleased at being on a panel with writers, but I couldn't help feeling like an impostor.

I began a novel, *Neanderthal*, during a stint as an editor in the New York office when I had some time on my hands. At first it was a diversion. I had read an article with some new information about those fascinating, extinct relatives of ours and I thought it would be fun to imagine a little band of them still existing in today's world and to bring them into conflict with our own devious, predatory tribe. I lathered the story with a lot of science, as accurate as I could make it, and so what I was working on, while technically a novel, was really commercial fiction. That's the term for a book that sells, and it's easier to do because you don't have to worry about being Faulkner every time you face a blank screen.

Soon I discovered a little gimmick. One day I complained to a friend and author, a fellow "hack" from the Nairobi press corps, that the work was going slowly, that I had been writing only a thousand words a day. He sat up like a bolt, downed his scotch and peered at me through a cloud of cigarette smoke. "One thousand words a day! That's terrific! Don't you realize? That's thirty thousand words a month. Three, four months and you've got a book." I did the math; he was right. I set my computer so that I could knock off the moment I hit a thousand words. The device worked. A momentous task had been cut down to bite sizes. No longer was I laboring to climb a mountain while staring at the snow-covered peak far above; instead I was climbing a single slope day after day until one day I would arrive at the summit. And one day I did. I began to feel like Molière's Bourgeois Gentilhomme learning that he has been speaking prose all along. The thought struck me that maybe I am a writer after all.

So, I thought, wouldn't it be interesting to commission a series by writers to let them talk about their craft? Maybe they would have similar tricks to impart. Maybe they could let some daylight in upon the magic. Where do they get their ideas? Or perhaps they should talk about literature. Or about reading—say, the general consensus that we are sinking into the abyss of an aliterate society. I drew up a list of writers that I wanted most to hear from (which was not the same, I was to learn, as a list of writers who might want to hear from me). I threw in some big names: Updike, Bellow, Doctorow. I added other names, younger writers, experimenters, radicals, miscreants. I went to PEN gatherings and moved from table to table signing up people like a Hollywood agent.

I learned a number of things. Not all writers want to talk about what they do. A lot of them do not meet deadlines. And unlike reporters, they do not accept assignments gracefully—they actually have to *want* to do it. Beware of interrupting a writer in the middle of his working day: if he appears to want to remain on the line long after you do, that's not a good sign. Some are perfectionists (one was deeply miffed by a misplaced comma). Some are vain (one cut his piece by three hundred words to make room for a picture). And all of them are human in one respect: they wanted to hear, right away, what you thought of their work.

The series has been exceedingly popular. One reason

might be that the writing stands above the ordinary fare of a daily newspaper. Another is probably the subjects, which tend toward the personal and wander over the private range of the imagination. And a third reason, I believe, is that many people have a secret urge to become writers themselves. All of our lives are stories. How many times have you heard someone say that she has a good book inside her, if only she could get it out?

Which reminds me of a saucy remark from a friend of my son's, an English teenager smitten with premature wit. Lent my first book for a plane ride home, he sent back a postcard in a hand that fairly chuckled: "I thought your book was good," he wrote. "They say everyone has a great book inside him. I look forward to yours."

But I digress. And my computer informs me that I have stayed too long—by twenty-six words.

WRITERS
ON
WRITING

A Literary Pilgrim
Progresses to the Past

~

André Aciman

What my dentist cried out one day after finally remov-
ing an unsuspected fourth nerve from one of my
molars comes to mind each time I try to understand myself
as a writer. Do I, as a writer, have what he called a "hidden
nerve"?

Don't all writers have a hidden nerve, call it a secret
chamber, something irreducibly theirs, which stirs their
prose and makes it tick and turn this way or that, and iden-
tifies them, like a signature, though it lurks far deeper than
their style, or their voice or other telltale antics?

A hidden nerve is what every writer is ultimately about.
It's what all writers wish to uncover when writing about
themselves in this age of the personal memoir. And yet it's
also the first thing every writer learns to sidestep, to disguise, as though this nerve were a deep and shameful secret
that needs to be swathed in many sheaths. Some don't
even know they've screened this nerve from their own gaze,
let alone another's. Some crudely mistake confession for

introspection. Others, more cunning perhaps, open tempting shortcuts and roundabout passageways, the better to mislead everyone. Some can't tell whether they're writing to strip or hide that secret nerve.

I have no idea to which category I belong.

As for a sheath, however, I'd spot mine in a second. It is place. I begin my inward journey by writing about place. Some do so by writing about love, war, suffering, cruelty, power, God or country. I write about place, or the memory of place. I write about a city called Alexandria, which I'm supposed to have loved, and about other cities that remind me of a vanished world to which I allegedly wish to return. I write about exile, remembrance and the passage of time. I write—so it would seem—to recapture, to preserve and return to the past, though I might just as easily be writing to forget and put that past behind me.

And yet my hidden nerve lies quite elsewhere. To work my way closer to it, I'd have to write about loss and feeling unhinged in provisional places where everyone else seems to have a home and a place, and where everyone knows what he wants, who he is and who he's likely to become.

My Alexandrians, however, have an unsteady foothold wherever they stand; they shift time zones, life passions, loyalties and accents with the unwieldly sense that the real world swims before them, that they are strangers in it, that they're never quite entitled to it. Yet peel this second sheath, and you'll find another.

I may write about place and displacement, but what I'm really writing about is dispersion, evasion, ambivalence: not so much a subject as a move in everything I write. I may write about little parks in New York that remind me of Rome and about tiny squares in Paris that remind me of

New York, and about so many spots in the world that will ultimately take me back to Alexandria. But this crisscrossed trajectory is simply my way of showing how scattered and divided I am about everything else in life.

I may never mention dispersion or evasion by name. But I write around them. I write away from them. I write from them, the way some people write around loneliness, guilt, shame, failure, disloyalty, the better to avoid staring at them.

Ambivalence and dispersion run so deep that I don't know whether I like the place I've chosen to call my home, any more than I know whether I like the writer or even the person I am when no one's looking. And yet the very act of writing has become my way of finding a space and of building a home for myself, my way of taking a shapeless, marshy world and firming it up with paper, the way the Venetians firm up eroded land by driving wooden piles into it.

I write to give my life a form, a narrative, a chronology; and, for good measure, I seal loose ends with cadenced prose and add glitter where I know things were quite lusterless. I write to reach out to the real world, though I know that I write to stay away from a world that is still too real and never as provisional or ambivalent as I'd like it to be. In the end it's no longer, and perhaps never was, the world that I like, but writing about it. I write to find out who I am; I write to give myself the slip. I write because I am always at one remove from the world but have grown to like saying so.

Thus I turn to Alexandria, the mythical home of paradox. But Alexandria is merely an alibi, a mold, a construct. Writing about Alexandria helps me give a geographical frame to a psychological mess. Alexandria is the nickname I give this mess. Ask me to be intimate, and I'll automatically start writing about Alexandria.

I'll write about diaspora and dispossession, but these big words hold my inner tale together, the way lies help keep the truth afloat. I use the word *exile*, not because I think it is the right term, but because it approximates something far more intimate, more painful, more awkward: exile from myself, in the sense that I could so easily have had another life, lived elsewhere, loved others, been someone else.

If I keep writing about places, it is because some of them are coded ways of writing about myself: like me, they are always somewhat dated, isolated, uncertain, thrust precariously in the middle of larger cities, places that have become not just stand-ins for Alexandria, but stand-ins for me. I walk past them and think of me.

Let me turn the clock back thirty years.

It is October 1968, and I've just arrived in New York City. Mornings are nippy. It's my second week here. I have found a job in the mailroom at Lincoln Center. During my rounds at 10:30 every morning the plaza is totally empty and its fountain silent. Here every day I am always reminded of my very early childhood, when my mother would take me for long walks along a quiet plantation road far beyond our home.

There is something serene and peaceful in this memory. I go out every morning knowing that as soon as I get a whiff of a nippy Manhattan breeze, I'll encounter the memory of those plantation mornings and the hand that held mine along these long walks.

Fast-forward more than two decades. It is 1992. On certain warm summer days at noon I go to pick up my mother on Sixtieth Street, where she still works as an office clerk.

We buy fruit and sandwiches on Broadway and walk awhile until we find a shady stone bench at Lincoln Center's Damrosch Park. At times I bring my two-year-old son, who'll scamper about, eating a spoonful, then run back to hide in between raised flowers beds.

Afterward he and I walk my mother back to her office; we say good-bye, then head toward Broadway to catch the bus across from a tiny park where Dante's statue stands. I tell him of Paolo and Francesca, and of cruel Gianciotto, and of Farinata the exile and Count Ugolino who starved with his children.

Dante's statue still reminds me of the tales I told my son then; it reminds me of this park and of other small parks I've since written about, and of how I felt guilty as a son, letting my mother hold so menial a job in her seventies, taking her out for a walk when it was clearly too warm for her, and how, to write a memoir about our life in Egypt, I had hired a full-time baby-sitter who was only too glad to have the time off whenever I'd take my son to lunches that I resented sometimes because they'd steal me from my desk. I think back to that summer and to my explosive snubs whenever my mother complained I'd arrived too late again.

One day, after losing my temper and making her cry at lunch, I went home and wrote about how she would sit in our balcony in Alexandria smoking a cigarette, and of how the wind had fanned her hair on the day she came to pick me up at school after someone had called home saying I had been suspended that day. Together we rode the tram downtown, naming the stations one by one.

Now, whenever I look back to those hot afternoons at Lincoln Center, I see two boys, me and my son, and I see my mother both as she was during those summer lunches in the

5

early '90s and as I remembered her on our walks along the plantation road two and a half decades earlier. But the one mother most clearly limned on those stone benches at Damrosch Park is the one riding the tram with me: serene, ebullient, carefree, catching the light of the sun on her face as she recited the names of the stations to me.

I did not lie about the names of the tram stations, but I did make up the scene about her coming to school that day. It doesn't matter. For this scene's hidden nerve lay somewhere else: in my wanting to stay home and write, in not knowing which mother I was writing about, in wishing she could be young once more, or that I might be her young boy again, or that both of us might still be in Egypt, or that we should be grateful we weren't.

Perhaps it had something to do with my failure to rescue her from work that day, which I'd inverted into her rescuing me from school; or perhaps with my reluctance to believe that an entirely invented scene could have so cathartic an effect, and that lies do purge the mind of mnemonic dead weight.

I don't know. Perhaps writing opens up a parallel universe into which, one by one, we'll move all of our dearest memories and rearrange them as we please.

Perhaps this is why all memoirists lie. We alter the truth on paper so as to alter it in fact; we lie about our past and invent surrogate memories the better to make sense of our lives and live the life we know was truly ours. We write about our life, not to see it as it was, but to see it as we wish others might see it, so we may borrow their gaze and begin to see our life through their eyes, not ours.

Only then, perhaps, would we begin to understand our

life story, or to tolerate it and ultimately, perhaps, to find it beautiful; not that any life is ever beautiful, but the measure of a beautiful life is perhaps one that sees its blemishes, knows they can't be forgiven and, for all that, learns each day to look the other way.

A Novelist's Vivid Memory Spins Fiction of Its Own

~

Russell Banks

One early March night in Boston, while on tour promoting a novel I'd recently published, I gave a reading at a theater across the street from the Coolidge Corner bookstore where in 1961 I was briefly employed, most unhappily, as a shipping clerk consigned to the basement. The theater was filled to overflowing, and the occasion was for me, these many years later, a grand occasion, a triumphant homecoming.

I told this to the audience before the reading, perhaps to personalize the by now nearly rote recitation, but more likely merely to flatter myself. Back in the winter of 1961, I said, I was a twenty-one-year-old dropout, a kid with little more than a fantasy that he was a writer, living in the Back Bay demimonde among poets and hustlers, artists and drug addicts, musicians and con men. I was literary, but not very literate, a late-arriving beatnik with a taste mainly for getting wasted.

Depressed, trapped in my bookstore basement cubicle

like Bartleby the Scrivener, I preferred not to, and had what today we would call a nervous breakdown. Back then all it meant was that I couldn't get myself to go to work one day, then the next, and the next, until I no longer had a job. I was running out of small money fast, was down to chump change. My life, all of life, seemed squalid and empty. I was a failure and hadn't even started trying yet.

One bleary morning I woke and decided that what I needed was solitude and time. And sunshine! For my writing, you understand, to become an artist. I bounced a couple of checks in the neighborhood and one dark and stormy night took off for Florida, hitching my way out of town. And ended up in Key West, where I rented a room in a tumbledown old building and wrote my first short stories, based, naturally, on the stories of Key West's most famous citizen, Papa Hemingway. That was how my life as a writer began.

I told this to the audience in Boston and then went on to read from my novel and afterward to sit at a table and sign books, until, near the end of the line, there came a gray-haired man with elaborate tattoos crawling up his arms and a soft cloth cap on his head. He leaned close to the signing table and in a filed-down voice said: "Russ, babe, it didn't go down that way. The way you said."

I recognized him instantly, a man from my distant past, a small-time gangster named Jocko. "You wanna know how it was, I'm across the street in the Tam. You get through with this signin' an' whatever, come over for a drink."

He'd been connected, I remembered, specializing in marijuana sales and debt collection and low-level physical violence. I'd been a little scared of Jocko but, because of his intelligence and wry streetwise cynicism, had liked hanging with him. I was beat, and Jocko was cool. Nervously—

maybe I kited those checks on him, and now he wants to collect, with interest—I said: "Wow, Jocko! What're you doing these days, man?"

"Little a this, little a that," he shrugged. "Same as always."

When you meet a witness to your distant past, your memory tends to improve. By the time I left the theater, I was remembering the girl who'd left me for another and that I had fled Boston, not to forge the conscience of my race in the smithy of my soul, but to protect my weepy eyes from the sight of a perfidious woman in the arms of her new love.

She was a lively college girl from Virginia and for six months had been slipping from her dormitory room on weekends to share my mattress on the floor and my night-life on the streets of Boston. We dreamed of marriage and children, for we were children of the 1950s, after all, and that's where sex led.

She'd given her protective parents a capsule description of the boy she'd fallen for, and they had disapproved of him. Understandably. Even I disapproved of him.

Thus it seemed both right and inevitable when, without warning, caught between following her heart and her heritage, she abandoned me for the scion of an old patrician Hudson Valley family, a Harvard boy with a future guaranteed to match his pedigreed past. I obviously had neither future nor past.

Crossing Brookline Avenue in the spring rain from the theater to the Tam, I thought of the girl with renewed fondness. She had long brown hair and a face like a Victorian cameo brooch, a perfect oval. She played the guitar and sang folk songs in coffeehouses, and she slept more peacefully than anyone I had ever known.

No matter how late we'd stayed up the night before, I always woke at dawn and stared brooding from the sooty window of my Back Bay room, depressed and usually hungover, while my darling floated through dreams of magnolias and wisteria till noon and woke rested and freshly thrilled to find me present in her otherwise charmed life. That's what I had lost.

Jocko said: "Man, you was cryin' over that dame. You didn't know what to do. I got pretty tired of it, so I finally said get outa Boston, man. Go to Florida.

"As you may recall, I was just back from Florida myself," he added. "Having been kicked outa Cuba when we was tryin' to bring strippers and gamin' back in. You remember, kid, I was the bodyguard for Rose La Rose." No one had called me kid in thirty years. "Rose was already over the hill, but we figured, what the hell, these guys are Communists, they'll never know the difference."

It was Jocko, then, and not Hemingway, who had said, Go South, young man. He'd given me the names of several of his associates in the Keys, gangsters working in Islamorada helping the CIA train Cubans for what turned out to be the Bay of Pigs invasion, and some other guys in Key West who worked at more innocent pastimes, providing American sailors with prostitutes and card games. It was all coming back now.

"I was like your mentor, kid. Your teacher. But, man, you was naive! Too naive to teach, if you wanta know the truth. And romantic! It wasn't art that made you lose your job at the bookstore. It was a broad. I remember you hitchin' outa town with your dumb backpack and all, and this stupid huntin' knife on your belt, and I'm thinkin', I'm tryin' to get this kid connected, I'm sendin' him to guys who carry automatic weapons, and he's got a New Hampshire huntin' knife on his belt!"

I thought it, but Jocko said it: "It's a good thing you became a writer, kid. You'da made a lousy gangster."

He was right, of course. Looking back, it seems clear that writing saved me from a life of crime. There wasn't much else available to me. I surely never would have worked my way up and out of the basement of that bookstore. No way I'd have married my girl, become a salesman, the store manager, a rising captain of the bookselling industry, my Virginia in-laws' pride.

I really was like Bartleby the Scrivener. Not Stephen Dedalus, not the young Hemingway. And if I had turned to crime, I'd have been woefully inept and surely would've ended up in jail or dead at a very young age, even for a gangster.

I asked Jocko why he'd hung around with all those poets and artists and musicians back then. "You were one scary dude, man," I said.

He said: "Yeah, well, artists are a lot like gangsters. They both know that the official version, the one everyone else believes, is a lie."

He was right about that, too.

To Engage the World More Fully, Follow a Dog

Rick Bass

I never set out to write a whole book about my dog Colter, much less two books, but he was such a force, such a marvelous animal and taught me so much—about hunting, certainly, but about barely controllable and indomitable passion as well—that in his absence my pen has been moving and even now has not yet ceased.

Ours was a complex relationship, certainly. I was forty-one years old before I was ever even asked the difference between caring for and admiring, even loving, one animal, such as a dog, like Colter, and hunting another animal, such as a grouse: using, in fact, that first animal, Colter, to lead you to the second in order that the two of you—dog and man, or dog and woman—might then endeavor to take the bird's life.

The why of the relationship is simple: a dog such as my great Colter can find a hidden bird—a pheasant, a sharp-tailed grouse, a bobwhite quail—where I cannot, where I would walk right on past. The why is easy: using a great dog like Colter is the most efficient, as well as most exhilarating, way to find the birds.

The dog's talents and enthusiasm—mania is perhaps the more accurate word—stretch your own tired and dull senses. When you are hunting with the dog, pursuing the thing the dog has been pursuing forever, the dog requires that you become more alert, more alive: more engaged, not only to landscape and quarry but to the dog's own responses to these things.

If the question is, however, why, if one admires the dog's talents and nearly as deeply admires the wild bird's qualities, does one participate in the nurturing of one and yet the pursuit, with the goal of rendering into food, of the other—well, I can't answer for the dog. But I can tell what it is like for me, when I am engaged fully in the hunt with a creature I've cared for and known for each day of the year, hunting on my home ground, land I live on or pass by almost every day of the year.

And perhaps in the telling of what it is like, this other why can be discovered, or seen. And even now considering the question, it seems to me not so much that there is a difference between the two—caring for the dog, but not for the bird—but rather the opposite, particularly when in the field, when dog, bird and hunter are braided together: converging, not separating.

The Spanish philosopher Ortega y Gassett said that in the realm of natural history (and what other kind is there?) the prey, with its flight, fairly summons the predator; that, as paraphrased by Thomas McIntyre, "animals thought of as game are not hunted by chance, but because in the instinctive depths of their natures, they have already foreseen the hunter (before he even enters the woods) and have, therefore, been shaped to be alert, suspicious, and eva-sive. . . . And again according to the philosopher, the only adequate response to a being that lives obsessed with avoid-ing capture is to try to catch it."

I'd agree with certain elements of this idea, particularly since I've never felt any inkling to hunt other predators—bears, lions, etc.—nor the largest mammals, like moose or elephants, which do not flee.

Each hunter, I think, has one particular species, or sort of species, whose manner and flight and habits and native landscape most speak to, and summon, him or her. (For me it is the upland birds, which crouch and then whir away fast. For others it is the white-tailed deer; for others, the elk. I think that each combination of hunter, landscape and quarry sounds a slightly different resonance in the heart of each individual hunter.)

If this is so, then all variances of bad behavior from hunters—or shooters, as I call them—as well as all puzzle-ment or disbelief or misunderstanding by nonhunters, as to why a hunter hunts, with or without a dog (the dog in the best instances an extension of the hunter's self, taking his or her senses a bit further than where they could travel otherwise), might result from the inability to reside, or under-stand what it is like to reside, within that personal summons.

Worst of all, I think, is the hunter or shooter who goes afield, and persists afield without an examining of these things: who hunts (or shoots) only to fill his or her bag, or to step outside him- or herself in order to view the picture he or she makes in that pursuit, rather than becoming lost in that summons, if indeed the mysterious twinings of blood and landscape and quarry and hunger and experience and dog and season and perhaps ten thousand other variables do combine in that person, as it is said they do in roughly 5 percent of our population, to elicit a summons in the first place.

I like being alone in the field, or with one or two good friends, keeping my eyes pretty much on the dog: shifting them from the landscape, to the dog, to my friend, back to the landscape.

Can I really explain what it is like, to reside in that place? Not really. I can only write about it. Another person without this same blood and experience could stand on the same hillside, behind the same dog pointing to the same hidden bird—awaiting the thunderous explosion of wings—but that person would not be me, would not be inside me.

What the summons is like is a thing more ineluctable than scent or any quarry. It is the essence of one's own blood imperative, being called into the world. I don't end up taking many wild birds. But the distance between their dark deep flesh, so hard-gotten, and the blander hues of food, plant or animal gotten in some other manner, known or unknown, is the distance that separates me from much of the rest of the world. It is the distance that allows me to fit, semismoothly, into my place in the world, and into the place inside myself: the place where I'm most comfortable and where the world makes the most sense.

It happens in the autumn. I step into that place. I become more myself and move toward, and after, the prey that was chosen for me long before I was born. The wild landscape becomes the widened boundaries of my life. The dog is my partner in this part of my journey.

Hidden Within Technology's Empire, a Republic of Letters

Saul Bellow

When I was a boy "discovering literature," I used to think how wonderful it would be if every other person on the street were familiar with Proust and Joyce or T. E. Lawrence or Pasternak and Kafka. Later I learned how refractory to high culture the democratic masses were. Lincoln as a young frontiersman read Plutarch, Shakespeare and the Bible. But then he was Lincoln.

Later when I was traveling in the Midwest by car, bus and train, I regularly visited small-town libraries and found that readers in Keokuk, Iowa, or Benton Harbor, Michigan, were checking out Proust and Joyce and even Svevo and Andrey Bely. D. H Lawrence was also a favorite. And sometimes I remembered that God was willing to spare Sodom for the sake of ten of the righteous. Not that Keokuk was anything like wicked Sodom, or that Proust's Charlus would have been tempted to settle in Benton Harbor, Michigan. I seem to have had a persistent democratic desire to find evidences of high culture in the most unlikely places.

For many decades now I have been a fiction writer, and from the first I was aware that mine was a questionable occupation. In the 1930s an elderly neighbor in Chicago told me that he wrote fiction for the pulps. "The people on the block wonder why I don't go to a job, and I'm seen puttering around, trimming the bushes or painting a fence instead of working in a factory. But I'm a writer. I sell to *Argosy* and *Doc Savage*," he said with a certain gloom. "They wouldn't call that a trade." Probably he noticed that I was a bookish boy, likely to sympathize with him, and perhaps he was trying to warn me to avoid being unlike others. But it was too late for that.

From the first, too, I had been warned that the novel was at the point of death, that like the walled city or the crossbow, it was a thing of the past. And no one likes to be at odds with history. Oswald Spengler, one of the most widely read authors of the early '30s, taught that our tired old civilization was very nearly finished. His advice to the young was to avoid literature and the arts and to embrace mechanization and become engineers.

In refusing to be obsolete, you challenged and defied the evolutionist historians. I had great respect for Spengler in my youth, but even then I couldn't accept his conclusions, and (with respect and admiration) I mentally told him to get lost.

Sixty years later, in a recent issue of the *Wall Street Journal*, I come upon the old Spenglerian argument in a contemporary form. Terry Teachout, unlike Spengler, does not dump paralyzing mountains of historical theory upon us, but there are signs that he has weighed, sifted and pondered the evidence.

He speaks of our "atomized culture," and his is a responsible, up-to-date and carefully considered opinion. He speaks of "art forms as technologies." He tells us that movies will soon be "downloadable"—that is, transferable from one computer to the memory of another device—and predicts that films will soon be marketed like books. He predicts that the near-magical powers of technology are bringing us to the threshold of a new age and concludes, "Once this happens, my guess is that the independent movie will replace the novel as the principal vehicle for serious storytelling in the 21st century."

In support of this argument, Teachout cites the ominous drop in the volume of book sales and the great increase in movie attendance: "For Americans under the age of 30, film has replaced the novel as the dominant mode of artistic expression." To this Teachout adds that popular novelists like Tom Clancy and Stephen King "top out at around a million copies per book," and notes, "The final episode of NBC's *Cheers*, by contrast, was seen by 42 million people."

On majoritarian grounds, the movies win. "The power of novels to shape the national conversation has declined," says Teachout. But I am not at all certain that in their day *Moby-Dick* or *The Scarlet Letter* had any considerable influence on "the national conversation." In the mid-nineteenth century it was *Uncle Tom's Cabin* that impressed the great public. *Moby-Dick* was a small-public novel.

The literary masterpieces of the twentieth century were for the most part the work of novelists who had no large public in mind. The novels of Proust and Joyce were written in a cultural twilight and were not intended to be read under the blaze and dazzle of popularity.

Teachout's article in the *Journal* follows the path generally taken by observers whose aim is to discover a trend.

"According to one recent study 55 percent of Americans spend less than 30 minutes reading anything at all. . . . It may even be that movies have superseded novels not because Americans have grown dumber but because the novel is an obsolete artistic technology.

"We are not accustomed to thinking of art forms as technologies," he says, "but that is what they are, which means they have been rendered moribund by new technical developments."

Together with this emphasis on technics that attracts the scientific-minded young, there are other preferences discernible: It is better to do as a majority of your contemporaries are doing, better to be one of millions viewing a film than one of mere thousands reading a book. Moreover, the reader reads in solitude, whereas the viewer belongs to a great majority; he has powers of numerosity as well as the powers of mechanization. Add to this the importance of avoiding technological obsolescence and the attraction of feeling that technics will decide questions for us more dependably than the thinking of an individual, no matter how distinctive he may be.

John Cheever told me long ago that it was his readers who kept him going, people from every part of the country who had written to him. When he was at work, he was aware of these readers and correspondents in the woods beyond the lawn. "If I couldn't picture them, I'd be sunk," he said. And the novelist Wright Morris, urging me to get an electric typewriter, said that he seldom turned his machine off. "When I'm not writing, I listen to the electricity," he said. "It keeps me company. We have conversations."

I wonder how Teachout might square such idiosyncrasies with his "art forms as technologies." Perhaps he would argue that these two writers had somehow isolated themselves from "broad-based cultural influence." Teachout has at least one laudable purpose: He thinks that he sees a way to bring together the Great Public of the movies with the Small Public of the highbrows. He is, however, interested in millions: millions of dollars, millions of readers, millions of viewers.

The one thing "everybody" does is go to the movies, Teachout says. How right he is.

Back in the '20s children between the ages of eight and twelve lined up on Saturdays to buy their nickel tickets to see the crisis of last Saturday resolved. The heroine was untied in a matter of seconds just before the locomotive would have crushed her. Then came a new episode; and after that the newsreel and *Our Gang*. Finally there was a western with Tom Mix, or a Janet Gaynor picture about a young bride and her husband blissful in the attic, or Gloria Swanson and Theda Bara or Wallace Beery or Adolphe Menjou or Marie Dressler. And of course there was Charlie Chaplin in *The Gold Rush*, and from *The Gold Rush* it was only one step to the stories of Jack London.

There was no rivalry then between the viewer and the reader. Nobody supervised our reading. We were on our own. We civilized ourselves. We found or made a mental and imaginative life. Because we could read, we learned also to write. It did not confuse me to see *Treasure Island* in the movies and then read the book. There was no competition for our attention.

One of the more attractive oddities of the United States is that our minorities are so numerous, so huge. A minority of millions is not at all unusual. But there are in fact millions of literate Americans in a state of separation from others of their kind. They are, if you like, the readers of Cheever, a crowd of them too large to be hidden in the woods. Departments of literature across the country have not succeeded in alienating them from books, works old and new. My friend Keith Botsford and I felt strongly that if the woods were filled with readers gone astray, among those readers there were probably writers as well.

To learn in detail of their existence you have only to publish a magazine like *The Republic of Letters*. Given encouragement, unknown writers, formerly without hope, materialize. One early reader wrote that our paper, "with its contents so fresh, person-to-person," was "real, nonsynthetic, undistracting." Noting that there were no ads, she asked, "Is it possible, can it last?" and called it "an antidote to the shrinking of the human being in every one of us." And toward the end of her letter our correspondent added, "It behooves the elder generation to come up with reminders of who we used to be and need to be."

This is what Keith Botsford and I had hoped that our "tabloid for literates" would be. And for two years it has been just that. We are a pair of utopian codgers who feel we have a duty to literature. I hope we are not like those humane do-gooders who, when the horse was vanishing, still donated troughs in City Hall Square for thirsty nags.

We have no way of guessing how many independent, self-initiated connoisseurs and lovers of literature have survived in remote corners of the country. The little evidence we have suggests that they are glad to find us, they are grateful. They want more than they are getting. Ingenious technology has failed to give them what they so badly need.

Pupils Glimpse an Idea, Teacher Gets a Gold Star

Anne Bernays

The first time I taught a writing class I was scared stiff. This was at a private school where I was filling in for a teacher who had left suddenly in the middle of the semester. Nothing I had done before—editing a magazine, publishing five novels—prepared me for trying to explain how I'd done it or, more daunting still, to translate what I worked at every day into curriculum.

I was a cook with nothing to measure with and no recorded recipes. Whatever I knew about constructing a piece of fiction lay in an unsorted jumble in what a shrink would call the unconscious but I prefer to think of as the cellar. This was the place I dipped into optimistically whenever I needed something.

If I had been asked how you build characterization or indicate motive, I would have been at a loss. I was like the centipede who, when asked which foot it moved first, froze. How could I teach others to write? Well, you can't really teach people how to write, can you? They either have it or they don't.

The head of the English department tried to reassure me: You can do it, therefore you can teach it. After all, the school was desperate. So teaching writing wasn't going to be like teaching calculus or even photography. Since it was considered one of the arts, a soft discipline, it wasn't necessary to have an advanced degree or even any training in the art of teaching. In other words, I was meant to wing it, to make it up as I went along.

The five teenagers I met in a bright and cozy classroom abutting a highway near the Charles River wore expectant faces. What to do? "Write a story," I said, aware of how incredibly hard it is to write a story, harder than a novel. Every piece must fit snugly; each word must carry the weight of three or four words spoken aloud, carelessly.

The students did their homework. They came back with stories about extraterrestrials or about young people waking up in the morning, walking barefoot across a cold floor while smelling the coffee brewing below, then into the bathroom to look at themselves in the mirror and wonder who they were and why they were here. It didn't take long to realize that they were making the same mistakes over and over again. I wasn't teaching them anything.

Suppose I asked them all to do the same exercise, like scales for a singer? So I made up an exercise as arbitrary and demanding as solfège, gave them a word limit, six hundred, and sent them off. I thought they would chafe at being reined in, having their imaginations severely clipped. But they surprised me by asking for another exercise and another. They were like first graders completing a page in an arithmetic workbook and getting a gold star for it.

Making up these prose drills forced me to start organizing and classifying the elements of fiction that lay in that messy heap. This was salutary for me, and I began to see that about half the student's battle is learning basic skills, while the other half involves tapping into imagination, memory and a singular view of life and the world, a view no one else shares until you put it into words.

My assignments sounded simple enough, but they were hard to bring off with style and conviction. One was an emotional childhood memory, to be told in the present tense, using the language and perceptions of a child, to be followed the next week by the same memory, this time in the past tense and from the point of view of an adult who, presumably, has learned something in the meantime.

From that time, 1975, I've taught writing at one place or another, always using exercises that focused on isolated elements of the craft, like dialogue, plot, point of view, characterization, revision, language. (The students hated the one in which they were not allowed to use any adjectives or adverbs, but it made them realize how strong verbs and nouns are, especially when they stand alone.) Along the way there were those suspicious of my black magic; the headmaster of another school described my fiction workshop in a memo to the faculty as "poison candy." I didn't know which to object to more strenuously, the poison part or the candy.

You can teach almost anyone determined to learn them the basics required to write sentences and paragraphs that say what you want them to say clearly and concisely. It's far more difficult to get people to think like a writer, to give up conventional habits of mind and emotion. You must be able to step inside your character's skin and at the same time to remain outside the dicey circumstances you have maneu-vered her into. I can't remember how many times I advised students to stop writing the sunny hours and write from where it hurts: "No one wants to read polite. It puts them to sleep."

The idea that people aren't always what they seem was a startling notion to more beginning students than I like to acknowledge. I thought everyone knew that a person who smiles all the time may very well have a troubled and even murderous heart. This in turn leads to an analysis of what it means to be a) cynical and b) skeptical, and how, if you're going to write fiction it's more productive to be b than a.

If you're going to write fiction that's even vaguely autobi-ographical—and which of us hasn't?—in trying to decide what to put in and what to leave out, don't consider what your friends, neighbors and especially your immediate fam-ily are going to think and/or say, assuming, that is, that they ever read what you write. You don't want to hurt people deliberately; if you've got the proper skills, you can disguise most people so they won't recognize themselves.

There's a sureness to good writing even when what's being written about doesn't make all that much sense. It's the sureness of the so-called seat of an accomplished horse-back rider or a sailor coming about in a strong wind. The words have both muscle and grace, familiarity and surprise. If forced to choose one writer of the twentieth century who has these qualities most abundantly, I would name Vladimir Nabokov, who makes me want to take back everything I said about adjectives, except that each of his is chosen as care-fully as an engagement ring: "On her brown shoulder, a raised purple-pink swelling (the work of some gnat) which I eased of its beautiful transparent poison between my long thumbnails and then sucked till I was gorged on her spicy blood."

You can't teach that kind of sureness; it come only after writing every day, sometimes for years. The stock questions— "How will I know when to stop?" "How much detail is enough?"—can only be answered by "You'll know," trusting that as they acquire skill their mean self-editors are developing real muscle.

You can't teach someone who is tone-deaf how to sing. But those people don't turn up for singing lessons. Students learn pretty fast whether or not they can carry a tune. When they can't, they leave the class.

And there's this to teaching: It's a public act. You're on, people listen to you, watch you, endow you with an authority you don't deserve. Most good teachers have a streak of the theatrical, myself not excluded. My mother wanted me to be a musical comedy actress-singer and to this end sent me to a celebrated singing teacher who had trained a good many Broadway and concert hall voices.

I took lessons from this woman until I appeared triumphantly as Papageno in my girls' school production of *The Magic Flute.* It was, I confess, a high point in my life almost as exhilarating as the sale of my first short story.

My most recurrent anxiety dream is not about writing but about getting up onstage and realizing I haven't learned my solo. The writer ultimately took over from the singer, and I'm not at all sorry about that. After forty-five or so the singing voice begins to thin and waver. A writer's voice, God willing, is clear and strong until she's carried out feet first.

Characters' Weaknesses
Build Fiction's
Strengths

Rosellen Brown

Many years ago, just after my first novel, *The Auto-biography of My Mother*, was published, I was having dinner in Cambridge, Massachusetts, with a friend who was a lawyer. In fact he was a very patient civil liberties lawyer whom I had consulted about a number of points of law when I was writing that book, in which the mother of the title is herself a civil liberties lawyer. He had brought to the restaurant a friend of his, a woman who was a recent Harvard Law School graduate, and in the course of conversation somehow it emerged—writers always seem to make sure it emerges—that I had just published a novel.

When I told the young woman the title of the book, I could see her face fall. Apparently she hadn't had enough experience with writers to know that our trade has taught us to be avid and heartbreakingly accurate readers of response, artists of innuendo, and there is nowhere you as audience can hide. So it was amply clear to me that this young woman did not think much of my book. She blundered into and out again of some rather vague and irrelevant adjectives that I think were meant to be complimentary. They were obviously far from the heart of the matter, her problem or mine.

Finally I said to her, "Clearly you didn't much enjoy my book," and I asked her to tell me why. This is a terrible thing to do to someone. I had made the rather simplistic assumption that as a lawyer she might have enjoyed seeing my lawyer at work, prying open many of the same assumptions and chipping at the complexities she lived with.

But her answer, although it was related, tapped a very different vein. After she got over her initial embarrassment at being disarmed—no, she hadn't much liked the book, but she hadn't thought it showed—she said: "Well, look, I'm a lawyer, too, and a woman, like your character, but"—and her expression became urgent as if she had clamped her hand to my arm—"the book was no help to me. It didn't tell me how I should live my life."

The innocence of her disappointment fascinated me. I myself, as creator of that book, had thought I had been addressing such tangles as the primordial relation between mother and daughter; one particular view of history and another; the difference between accident and intention; the question of where responsibility and blame might lie for the satisfactions of a life, especially as a mother and daughter might feel that responsibility.

It's a book about a brilliant, difficult, rigid mother whose social conscience is better developed than what we might call her "mothering skills," and her withered flower child of a daughter who's lived her life in this woman's heavy shadow. In the end, when they struggle over who will protect the daughter's child, everyone loses.

I had also hoped, more simply, that I had presented in a palpable way the feel of a particular set of lives in a particular time and place, both of them facing an assortment of moral quandaries, and that I had done so in convincing, perhaps, if I was lucky, even in moving voices. Instead, I was appalled to discover that I had readers who had approached my novel with the same desperate hunger for correction with which they would open "Outwitting the Female Fat Cell" or "Women Who Make Bad Choices." If any people needed how-to books to put their souls on the straight and narrow, it was my own flawed and searching characters.

As a novelist, it seemed sufficient to know what the questions are and then to represent recognizable men, women and children lighted by those illuminations that are human, not divine, thus never, like a season ticket to a ballpark, transferable. "Look how you live, my friends," said Chekhov, who neither condemned nor averted his eyes. "What a pity it is to live that way."

Yet when you are finished seeing a Chekhov play or reading a story of his, you have recognized brothers and sisters in bewilderment and hope, and perhaps you feel less alone for a while on your own. I have a hard time imagining that we would still be staging or reading a Chekhov whose characters were always more busy, cheerful and resourceful than we are. But many of us are not so hungry to annex the writer as guidance counselor; we do not, like the Harvard Law School graduate, expect a novel to be a kind of AAA strip map to guide us safely through the uncharted territory of the psyche. To me, all reading is escape reading. To assume the lives of fiction's more interesting characters—their needs, their enthusiasms, their turns of thought—is to be freed of my all-too-familiar self for a while, to be on the most intimate terms with people who intrigue me exactly because they are not me.

But there is a habit that's cousin to the urgent quest for role models common to many readers that is even more maddening. Everyone who attends a book group has run into it, not to mention those of us who are periodically subjected to the whims of impatient reviewers. It is the sentence that begins approximately, "I didn't like the book because X was irritating." Or: "Oh, I didn't finish it. When Y did Z, I just threw the book across the room." (Some readers are passionate, even athletic, in their likes and dislikes.)

Informed that my characters are not peerless in their virtue or that they sometimes make horrendous decisions, I would say (if only the complainant could hear), "Tell me something I don't know." I made the characters, set them in motion, gave them their problems. In return for that effort, what I want to know is not whether, like a focus group, my readers approve but rather: "Does this action or attitude seem plausible to you? Does it represent some reality you can recognize?"

Because for me it's usually when a character begins to be thorny that he or she turns interesting. Do we reject Lear because he bungles his fateful moment? Do we condemn Gurov in Chekhov's *Lady with Lapdog* because he's a rake: philandering, insincere, guilty of seducing an innocent married woman into an affair that is probably going to cause many people a good deal of pain? Though Jane Austen's Elizabeth is a delight, her Emma is not. Neither does George Eliot's Dorothea make the best of marital choices. Sue Bridehead literally frustrates Jude the Obscure into his grave. So on and so forth.

I'm obviously not talking about monstrous misbehavior

here: the antihero of *Notes from Underground* or the killer in *American Psycho*. I'm interested in what I'd call ordinary bad behavior, the kind most of us indulge in all too frequently despite our best intentions.

The list of our emotional shortfalls is a long one for most of us; and it is only in novels of romantic fantasy, Gothic or contemporary, in which people wear much better clothes than ours and live in more glorious digs, that the emotional warts and wrinkles can be airbrushed away. The whitewash is done with far greater subtlety by more serious novelists when they wrap things up a shade too neatly, when they bestow on their characters terrible challenges that would leave deep scars in "real life," then pat them lovingly on the head rather than do them any lasting damage.

In my newest novel, *Half a Heart*, one of my characters, Miriam, is a white woman, the other, Veronica, her biracial teenage daughter from whom she was separated by the politics of black power in the '60s. The story revolves around the awkwardness and suspicion that shadows their reunion after seventeen years.

An early reviewer condemned my characters for not having figured out how to pull off this very difficult meeting with sufficient grace; watching them, she wrote, was like watching an emotional train wreck. To which I find myself responding: "I worked so hard on setting up that train wreck, introducing surprises on the track, unexpected weather, insufficient trust and unacknowledged emotions. What would have been the point had it all gone swimmingly? That would have been a dream." There is hope for this relationship at the end of my book, but it is not a promise.

Another reviewer said that at some point along the way she just wanted to spritz my character Miriam with ice water and tell her to go get a job. Well, so did I. Why does a criticism of a character have to become criticism of the book that contains her, when in fact that very failure of Miriam's is part of what the book is about?

After the loss of her child, Miriam, an ex-activist turned suburban matron, has been hopelessly becalmed, I think that's the best word for it. She is torpid, mildly, chronically depressed, moored in a life she never intended to choose for herself: her mother's life, minus her mother's energy and style. So since I designed her this way, a reader's impatience with her hardly comes as a surprise to me. To have made her instantly adequate to her situation would have made a heroine when in fact I was trying to walk with her through the painful first footsteps toward some kind of self-knowledge.

Yet, in the late '70s, the admirable novelist and critic John Gardner perverted the question of what fiction is for by suggesting that it actually ought to be pulling a heavy ethical and didactic load. There was, in contemporary literature, he wrote, "too much flash, not enough representation, not enough morality."

He went on to say that if the artist could find no pleasure in what happy human beings have found good for centuries—children and dogs (I mean it), peace, wealth, comfort, love, hope and faith—"then it is safe to hazard that he has not made a serious effort to sympathize and understand." He admonished us not to give sustained attention to the afflicted and despairing—he called them freaky— because to worship the unique, the unaccountable and freaky is, if we're consistent, "to give up the right to say to our children, Be good."

I beg to differ. To be reminded of the difficulty of things— to be taught the inescapable complexity of the world—

frequently makes one unfit to be a smiling moral arbiter. The writer may organize the chaos of our lives a little, which makes the questions clearer, but that has nothing to do with the provision of reductive answers or people who always respond "appropriately."

I have nothing against lovable characters; there are a great many wonderful ones out there, and no one ought to go out of his or her way to deny a character's best qualities for the sake of being called "uncompromising, hard-edged." But our first obligation is to create interesting, suggestive, realistic, possibly even challenging situations, set our character down in them and see where they go. Which may not be the way you wish they could; rather it is the way, given who they are, they must go.

I rarely have any idea how my people are going to react before they're in the thick of things, trying to find their way out. If I were to sand down their edges, I'd be making dolls; if I let their texture stay rough and their responses dangerously lifelike, I dare to think I might have resonant characters pocked and shadowed with complexity.

I suppose the first realistically flawed actors on the narrative stage were in the Bible. There is precious little perfection of character in the Old Testament. The miscreants may be punished, but few achieve what we in our century call self-awareness or self-consciousness, let alone remorse for their sins. Stories of malfeasance, starting with Adam, Eve and the serpent, have always been far better, if more provisional, ways than spotlessness of soul to stir an audience to attention and meditation.

How Can You Create Fiction When Reality Comes to Call?

~

Carolyn Chute

This is a very personal and uplifting story of my life as a writer. I will include intimate confessions. The following is a typical day in my life.

Eyes open up. Birds singing outside window. Oh, yes, and there is the husband. X-rated stuff happens. (Delete details.)

Must go out with dogs. They have a dog door and a half-acre fenced in with trees and a little brook, but that isn't good enough. . . . No, they have to have me go with them, so we can be a pack together.

Typewriter with page 1,994 of novel screams from another room: I WANT YOU.

I am scrambling to get dressed because the dogs are waiting at the foot of the stairs for the pack thing, which hasn't happened yet. They are hopping up and down. These are Scottish terriers with short legs, big heads, beady eyes and beards, and when I look at them, I melt and will do anything they want.

But at this moment I am still scrambling to get dressed, and the typewriter is starting to really scream and kind of whimper from the other room. A truck pulls up in the yard, a member of our political group, one of those working-class politics groups you hear so much about.

Bang! Bang! Bang! This is knuckles knocking on door.

Dogs charge the door.

Cuckoo clock coo coos six times.

Husband is now scrambling to get dressed.

Phone does not ring. Its bell is broken. It never rings. Thank heavens.

Typewriter is starting to gasp and moan.

All dressed, I race down the attic stairs and the pack is racing around, the dogs throwing themselves at the door behind which the guest stands.

The dishes heaped in the sink make no sound. No screams. No barking. But they have one of those profound presences. I am a person who can't teach writing or make a living in any public way, as I get confused when interrupted or overstimulated. In a classroom or crowded room, I all but blank out.

So my only income is from novels. This should explain the absence of dishwasher, clothes dryer, running hot water, electricity in all rooms, health insurance and other such luxuries. The Scotties we got through friends. So don't go rolling your eyes about those "expensive Scotties."

Husband opens front door for guest, as I head out the back door with the pack.

Pack does its thing, racing around, checking chipmunk holes, sniffing guest's truck to see what the news is from the outside world. It is a beautiful morning, and everything smells sweet.

Returning to the house, I close dogs in another room, so they won't bother the guest, who is sitting in a rocking chair with tea and telling about how upset he is with the latest bad thing the corporations and government (same thing) have done to us. (I will delete all his words here in order to keep this an uplifting and cheery article.)

Upstairs the typewriter is squealing and howling.

The dishes are deathly quiet.

I set the water kettles on the stove to heat, for dishes and baths and to get oatmeal started. Fetch the broom.

I get out the heartworm pills and line them up on the sideboard. (That's what us old Mainers call what you all call a counter.)

The guest is really upset and depressed. I sweep the broom around his chair and listen, and the husband is talking too about his troubles. He has plenty of troubles, too, as he is like me, not a marketable person.

Nowadays you are supposed to be marketable. Or you are unmarketable. Within the marketable group there are the house slaves (professional class) and the field slaves (working class). But some of us don't even make it to the auction block. So we are pretty upset. This might be taking this article out of the "uplifting" into the "uh-oh," so I'll switch now to how pretty the birds sound at the windows.

Guest leaves after another cup of tea.

Dogs line up for their heartworm pills.

Clock coo coos seven times.

Typewriter screams.

I do some dishes and take my bath and clock coo coos eight times and typewriter screams, and one of the Scotties starts to have a grand mal seizure. I hold her so she won't smash her skull on the floor.

Truck pulls up in the yard. Another guest, this a person who has read my book (the one with all the violence and class rage), and she comes in and sits in a rocker after we drive all the barking dogs out the dog door, except for the one that is dizzy and wet from her seizure, Florence, who I hold.

Husband goes out to split wood. Person tells me her name again and how hard she and her husband work, and yet they are losing everything and experiencing depression and rage, which they never experienced before. They have always been able to "keep up."

Typewriter screams.

I hear nine coo coos.

"Tea?" I ask the guest.

I hold Florence under one arm, make the tea.

Husband rushes in and tells me that Helen has been eating dirt again. This could mean an emergency trip to the vet's to have her pumped out. Helen is one of the Scotties.

By the time there are ten coo coos, guest has left. Dogs are lying around on the rockers. Husband has gone to town for the mail.

I finish hanging the laundry and go up to the typewriter and sit there, holding my head trying to quiet my head. You see, I can't just switch from life mode to writer mode. Usually it takes three days to get into the writer mode. Three days of quiet nonlife mode, lots of coffee and no interruptions.

Writing is like meditation or going into an ESP trance, or prayer. Like dreaming. You are tapping into your unconscious. To be fully conscious and alert, with life banging and popping and cuckooing all around, you are not going to find your way to your subconscious, which is a place of complete submission. Complete submission.

I open my eyes. I look at the page. I type a couple of lines. Pop! The "n" breaks off the daisy wheel.

These daisy wheels are $30 apiece! My old well-made typewriter had one daisy wheel, which lasted eleven years. But this is a new typewriter. The cheesy typewriters they make now use three daisy wheels a day. My mind abandons writer mode. I am now in crisis mode again. Ninety dollars a day for daisy wheels for a person who makes $2 an hour (what I figure I make) is pretty ugly.

UPS truck pulls up. Dogs hurtle out the dog door into their pen and throw selves against the fence wire to show the UPS man what will happen to him if he comes in the house. I run downstairs and out, so I can sign for the packages. Eight galleys from eight publishers wanting eight blurbs. Blurbs are those little positive-sounding quotes on the backs of books. I am not much of a reader. No time. It takes me two to six months to read a book, so these guys are definitely barking up the wrong tree.

UPS truck heads out and down the long dirt road and away.

I start back up the attic stairs to the gasping weeping typewriter, and husband arrives home with mail. Three more galleys in the mail, plus twenty letters and cards, most of which are urgent, or at least requiring a letter in return. Not many bills. Just our one huge mortgage on the house that we had to take out in order to eat.

Clock coo coos.

I remember a call I have to make, so I dial the phone. All I get is an answering machine.

Car pulls in the yard. A whole carload of family. Including a baby who is about ten months old and laughs at everything. He's kind of bald. His father holds him on his knee, so he can get a good view of all of us sitting in the circle of rocking chairs. The baby's mother tells how she's job hunting. Everything is a temp job, low pay, no bennies.

Baby laughs.

Grandmother says her husband, who is at work at the moment, is afraid his union is going to get busted.

Baby laughs.

The father, who is unemployed for not being marketable, is quiet. He adores this baby and keeps whispering stuff in the baby's ear that makes the baby laugh.

Typewriter screams in the room overhead.

Another carload of people. Neighbors rush in upset. The Drug Warriors have busted another neighbor for growing enough grass for just him and his brother to smoke. SWAT team nearly choked his naked wife (well, partially naked) and himself (he was wearing long johns) and is now seizing his house, after they stole all his savings, and he may go to prison for twelve years. The law guys are trying to scare his wife into testifying against him. You know, the usual. Telling her she'll lose her kids, etc.

Baby is laughing. So cute.

"Have a seat," I tell the new guests, and I set a match under the tea kettle.

I try the phone again. I get an answering machine.

Clock coo coos twelve times.

I sneak upstairs and make the bed and put away some clothes. My head feels fuzzy.

Another truck pulls up in the yard. It's our old friend who lived in his truck for years and finally has a little piece of land with an old school bus to live in, but the town says it is against codes, and they are trying to terrorize him and kick him out because a bus is considered dangerous.

The baby laughs.

"Have a seat."

"Can you go to the trial Tuesday?" a guests asks me.

"Of course," I answer. "We need to support our neighbors."

Another neighbor arrives.

Clock coo coos.

Typewriter is thumping on the ceiling above.

"Have a seat," I tell the newest guest.

"Legislature is trying to get death penalty passed," new guest tells me.

Baby laughs.

"Of course, rich people who kill through corporations and their poisons and fossil fuels and dangerous working conditions won't get the death penalty," neighbor says with a sigh, sips her tea. "This is for all us regular folks when we flip out."

We all look at the baby. He didn't catch this last remark. He's having his diaper changed while on his father's knees. I always am amazed at how that is done. I never mastered that knees method with my own baby and grandbabies.

Everyone leaves.

The mail, not all opened yet, is starting to make noises. Like the typewriter.

I try the phone again. I get the answering machine.

I figure I'd better feed the husband. He's out splitting wood again and looking thin. The stove is broke. I make a soup and toss a little store-bought bread on his bread plate.

I try the phone again.

Clock coo coos.

Dogs are coaxing to do the walk thing again, pack mode.

After the meal and the walk and three more times on the phone and Florence has another seizure, I go up to the typewriter. I sit awhile trying to quiet my head. I type a couple of sentences, and another $30 daisy wheel bites the dust.

I hear another vehicle in the yard. Just someone visiting the husband, a guy from town bringing him flags for his cemetery work.

But I can't concentrate with anybody around, so I figure I'll look at the mail. IRS wants paperwork. Which reminds me, we need to register the truck. About five letters from people doing short story collections who want a short story cheap, and a literacy group in Washington state would like me to fly out at my own expense and do a reading to help them raise money. Political mail. Emergencies. No checks. Nothing even like a check. Mean reviews. People who say my work has too much working-class rage.

Clock coo coos.

Car pulls up. Husband is gone out to do errands, so I herd the barking, snarling dogs out the dog door and usher the guest in. It's our friend Pete. Labor organizer, historian and professional troublemaker. He finds his favorite rocker while I make tea.

"I'm here to give you a test," he tells me with a chuckle. He proceeds to ask me questions about the making of the Constitution, like what percent of the population in 1776 was slaves and indentured servants and other people not considered human by "the Fathers."

"Ninety-five percent," I say.

He grunts unhappily. "You know too much."

The typewriter screams.

Clock coo coos four times.

"How's your book coming along?" Pete asks.

I laugh.

From Echoes Emerge
Original Voices

~

Nicholas Delbanco

R ecently I've been preparing a course for the fall semester, "Strategies in Prose." My writing students, a cohort
of fiction writers in the MFA program at the University of
Michigan, will read modern masterworks like *The Good
Soldier, To the Lighthouse, As I Lay Dying, A Farewell to Arms*
and *Ulysses.* As readers we will focus on aspects of technique, and the strategy for written assignments is that of
emulation, the close copy and pastiche.

I've taught a version of this class before, both to undergraduate and graduate students, and the results have been
remarkable. To engage in imitation is to begin to understand what originality means.

I'm hoping for additional language in the mode of Joyce
or Faulkner, for paragraphs that Ford or Woolf might
well have drafted and cut. While reading Hemingway, for
instance, we might take the final rain-drenched scene of *A
Farewell to Arms* and see what would have happened to the
mood of its conclusion if the weather that day had been

bright. Or if, instead, it had snowed. What would happen to the dinner scene at Woolf's Ramsay family table if the fare were not a boeuf en daube that "partook . . . of eternity" but pigs' trotters in wax paper or a fresh-caught trout?

We'll alter intonation, so that Joyce's Stephen Dedalus will hail from the Deep South; we'll give Faulkner's Anse Bundren the Irish accent of Leopold Bloom. We'll make Ford's Edward Ashburnham take a walk with Woolf's Lily Briscoe and see who proposes to whom. Much of this results in parody, of course, and it requires a tongue lodged in cheek, but I want to release young writers from the foredoomed expectation that their work must prove original. I want them to focus on manner, not matter, to study our great predecessors in an attempt to analyze not so much subject as style.

It's my conviction, moreover, that the two are inextricable, that Hemingway's short sentences stand in more than merely stylistic opposition to Faulkner's long ones. In the former, things are separable; in the latter, linked. We can tell the way a writer thinks by looking at his or her desire to use, say, the apposite comma or, as a sentence nears completion, the subordinate clause.

A system of values attaches to style. In *To the Lighthouse*, for example, the protagonist dies in a parenthesis, yet Virginia Woolf's decision to excise Mrs. Ramsay from the text in such a manner has as much to do with the conventions of her syntax as it does with her sense of mortality.

A characteristic device in the punctuation of Ford Madox Ford is the ellipsis, and this tells the reader something about what's unsayable or, in a scene, unsaid. There's an important difference, clearly, between a character whose mode is associative, digressive, trailing off into silence . . .

and one who ends his sentence fragment with exclamation points!

If art is an act of mimesis, a mirror held to nature, then it follows as the night the day that what we write must be impersonation, a way of tricking out twenty-six letters in order to ape "reality." That thing in quotes. We do this unconsciously always, sometimes consciously, in a kind of infection by inflection, a nearly viral transmission of a worldview via words. And in this forward-facing moment at the end of the millennium it seems we've acquired the Janus-faced habit of also looking back.

Michael Cunningham's prize-winning book *The Hours* is an extended act of imitation, that sincerest form of flattery; he enters the world both of Clarissa Dalloway and her creator, Woolf. *Shakespeare in Love* is highly allusive, a comedic tip of the cap to the language of Elizabethan England; the joke of *Romeo and Ethel and the Pirate's Daughter* requires prior knowledge of *Romeo and Juliet.* Patrick O'Brian's Aubrey and Maturin novels constitute an almost uninterrupted foray into the imaginative discourse of a world at war two hundred years ago, and large swatches of the story pay homage to Jane Austen or borrow from naval accounts. And these are just the iceberg's tip; present examples abound.

In other forms of performance we take repetition for granted, and personal expressiveness may even be a mistake. The members of a dance troupe must follow their choreographer's lead, moving in trained unison, and woe betide that member of the string section of an orchestra who chooses an exotic bowing.

The apprentice in an artist's shop might have mixed paint for years or learned to dado joints for what must have felt like forever; only slowly and under supervision could he approach the artifact as such. The French luthier J. B. Vuillaume took his pattern for stringed instruments unabashedly from his much-admired predecessor Stradivarius. This is not forgery so much as emulation, a willing admission that others have gone this way before.

Imitation is deeply rooted as a form of cultural transmission; we tell our old stories again and again. The bard in training had to memorize long histories verbatim, saying or singing what others had sung. In the oral formulaic tradition, indeed, the whole point was retentiveness; the impulse toward individual expression is a recent and a possibly aberrant one in art.

In this regard at least the early authors had it easier, had fewer doubts. They would have found nothing shameful in prescribed subjects or in avoiding the first-person pronoun. Since the stuff of the epic was constant, the apprentice could focus on style. A copyist must pay the kind of close attention to the model that a counterfeit does, and though such results may not be art, they are, when successful, real proof of technique.

It's possible, in other words, that the problem is not what to write but how to write it, and that a great weight can be lifted from young writers' shoulders if subject matter is predetermined, not something they need to invent.

Nor is signature important. The bulk of our literature's triumphs have been collective or anonymous. Who can identify the authors of the Bible, the *Ramayana*, *Beowulf*? More to the point, who cares? The *Iliad* and *Odyssey* are by an unknown bard, as are, for all practical purposes, the plays of Shakespeare. This is not to say that these works don't display personality—the reverse is more nearly true—but rather that the cult of personality should fade. It, too, is recent and, I think, aberrant; it has nothing to do with the labor of writing as such.

All this conjoins with the nature of language and our presumed literacy: a native familiarity with English that more often than not breeds contempt. No one presumes to give a dance recital without having first mastered the rudiments of dance, to perform Mozart before playing scales or to enter a weight-lifting contest without first hoisting weights. Yet because we've been reading since age five, we blithely assume we can read; because we scrawled our signature when six, we glibly aspire to write.

So one task of the teacher is to point out antecedents. "Tom, you might want to look at what Dick did with this plot device; Harriet, you might (re)read the novel by X, which your Y appears to follow." And more often than not the student has no notion that it's been tried before. Often the apprentice has not seen the model he or she has somehow come to imitate, and there's a way in which such ignorance is bliss, a precondition of the imagination engaged. Yet Ezra Pound's injunction "Make it new" predicates some knowledge of what was yesterday's news.

Therefore my students in September will look at the use of incantatory repetition, not the meaning of the snowstorm in *The Dead*. We'll study image clusters in Virginia Woolf, and the way the lighthouse looks to the separate characters who look at it, and why a sentence that has commas differs from one that does not. By semester's end these writers may not know the map of Dublin or the population of Yoknapatawpha County, but they will know—or the course will have failed—in what ways Hemingway's good soldier talks differently from Ford's.

Originality is rare indeed, not subject to instruction; and in any case it's not the purpose of "Strategies in Prose." Still, I expect that, having studied and absorbed these inimitable voices, their own voices will start to emerge.

The first phrase of what follows is the first of *The Good Soldier*, the last the last of *Ulysses*. The speaker of the second sentence is Faulkner's troubled Vardaman, and the third sentence of this brief pastiche belongs to a bitter Jake Barnes. Each of the words deployed are Anglo-Saxon in their origin, not Latinate; the longest have two syllables, yet authorial intention, tone, alters altogether from first to last:

This is the saddest story I have ever heard.

My mother is a fish.

Yes, isn't it pretty to think so.

yes I said yes I will Yes.

Quick Cuts: The Novel Follows Film into a World of Fewer Words

~

E. L. Doctorow

The effect of a hundred years of filmmaking on the practice of literature has been considerable.

As more than one critic has noted, today's novelists tend not to write exposition as fully as novelists of the nineteenth century. Where the first chapter of Stendahl's *Red and the Black* (1830) is given over to the leisurely description of a provincial French town, its topographic features, the basis of its economy, the person of its Mayor, the Mayor's mansion, the mansion's terraced gardens and so on, Faulkner's *Sanctuary* (1931) begins this way: "From beyond the screen of bushes which surrounded the spring, Popeye watched the man drinking."

The twentieth-century novel minimizes discourse that dwells on settings, characters' CVs and the like. The writer finds it preferable to incorporate all necessary information in the action, to carry it along in the current of the narrative, as is done in movies.

Of course there are nineteenth-century works, Mark

49

Twain's *Tom Sawyer*, for example ("'Tom?' No answer."), that jump right into things, and perhaps American writers have always been disposed to move along at a snappier pace than their European counterparts. But the minimal use of exposition does suppose a kind of filmic compact between writer and reader, that everything will become clear eventually.

Beyond that, the rise of film art is coincident with the tendency of novelists to conceive of compositions less symphonic and more solo voiced, intimate personalist work expressive of the operating consciousness. A case could be made that the novel's steady retreat from realism is as much a result of film's expansive record of the way the world looks as it is of the increasing sophistications of literature itself.

Another crossover effect has to do with film's major device, the instantaneous reposition in space and time: the cut. Writers today derive all sorts of effects from scanting the interstitial explanations or transitions that get their story from one character to another, or their characters from one place to another, or from yesterday to next year. More daring uses of discontinuity have occurred from violations of the grammatical protocols of person or tense.

But after a hundred years or so it may be that movies can do nothing more for, or to, literature than they have already done. By now film has begun to affirm its essentially nonliterate nature and to make of its conventions an art form detached and self-contained, like painting.

Movies began in silence. The early filmmakers learned to convey meaning apart from the use of language. For the most part the title cards of the silent films only nailed down the intelligence given to the audience nonverbally. (Young couple on porch swing at night. He removes a ring from his vest pocket. He gazes into her eyes. Title card: "Milly, will you be my wife?")

In the modern audible feature film, especially as made by Hollywood, spoken dialogue tends more and more to function as the old title cards of the silents. The genre of the film is indicated with the portentous opening credits. The beginning shots site the film and identify its time period. A given scene is lighted and the camera is positioned to create mood or inform the audience as to how it is to regard what it is seeing, how serious or unserious the story may be, how objectively we may regard the characters, how intimately we are being asked to share their adventures.

The film stock is color coordinated with its subject. The actors are dressed, and their hair is cut or coiffed, to indicate age, economic class, social status, education and even degree of virtue. They're directed to demonstrate their characters' states of mind with bodily attitudes, gestures, facial expressions and the movements of their eyes. Given all this, the weight of the scene is carried nonverbally. What is seen and felt is a signifying context for any words actually spoken. In some of today's film dramas 95 percent of a scene's meaning is conveyed before a word is uttered; 98 percent if you add music.

Of course recent filmmakers—Eric Rohmer, for example, or Louis Malle—have made highly verbal films. And as a generalization, the assemblage of visual effects that make of dialogue a capstone is less true of comedy. The art of the television sitcom, for example, is highly verbal. Its standing sets, and its inclination to celebrate character, provide the impetus for wordplay, gags and verbal economies that can verge on the aphoristic. On the other hand the sitcom's mostly interior scenes and its limited scope for camera setups suggest it is closer to a filmed stage play than it is to movies.

In the 1930s and '40s, when stage plays and books were a major source of film scripts, the talkies were talkier (as adaptations of Shakespeare are still). Films of that period were, by comparison with today's products, logorrheic. Even action films, the Bogart film noir, the Errol Flynn swash-buckler, abounded with dialogue. Now, after a century of development, the medium of film generates its own culture. Its audience is as schooled in its rhythms and motifs and habits of being as Wagnerians are in der Nibelungen. Films work off previous films. They are genre referential and can be more of what they are by nature.

Literary language extends experience in discourse. It flowers to thought with nouns, verbs, objects. It thinks. That is why the term *film language* may be an oxymoron. Film deliterates thought; it relies primarily on an association of visual impressions or understandings. Moviegoing is an act of inference. You receive what you see as a broad band of sensual effects that evoke your intuitive nonverbal intelli-gence. You understand what you see without having to think it through with words.

What shall we make of this? Today, at the end of the cen-tury, film is ubiquitous. There are more movies than ever. They are in theaters, on television; they are cabled, video-taped, CD'd and DVD'd. They are sent around the world by satellite transmission; they are dubbed and translated and available from all their periods for consumers to choose as books are chosen from the library. Their enormous popular-ity reaches all classes and all levels of education. And their primary producers are major entertainment conglomerates that put lots of money into them and expect even more money in return.

It is not that great and important films will no longer be made. But one can imagine a merger of film esthetics and profit-making incentives that, apart from the efforts of this or that serious and principled filmmaker, effects a culture of large, beautifully dressed, tactically pigmented, stimulating and only incidentally verbal movies that excite predetermined market tastes and offer societal myths that slightly vary with each recycling: films composed artfully from the palette of such basic elements as car drive-ups, interiors, exteriors, faces, chases and explosions.

Just as significant for the culture of the future may be the declining production costs of computerized, digitally made movies. It is not hard to understand the lure to the creative young when making a film will be as feasible as writing a story.

That pictograms, whether corporately or privately produced, may eventually unseat linguistic composition as the major communicative act of our culture is a prospect I find only slightly less dire than global warming.

Some of the most thoughtful if not ingenious criticism written today is written by critics of film who, often as not, address themselves to work that is hardly worth their attention. The most meretricious or foolish movie will elicit a cogent analysis. Why? It may be a film's auspices that obligate the critics. But it may be that, however unconsciously, they mean to reaffirm or defend print culture by subjecting the nonliterate filmgoing experience, good or bad, to the extensions of syntactical thought.

Two Languages in Mind, but Just One in the Heart

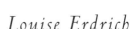

Louise Erdrich

For years now I have been in love with a language other than the English in which I write, and it is a rough affair. Every day I try to learn a little more Ojibwe. I have taken to carrying verb conjugation charts in my purse, along with the tiny notebook I've always kept for jotting down book ideas, overheard conversations, language detritus, phrases that pop into my head. Now that little notebook includes an increasing volume of Ojibwe words. My English is jealous, my Ojibwe elusive. Like a besieged unfaithful lover, I'm trying to appease them both.

Ojibwemowin, or Anishinabemowin, the Chippewa language, was last spoken in our family by Patrick Gourneau, my maternal grandfather, a Turtle Mountain Ojibwe who used it mainly in his prayers. Growing up off reservation, I thought Ojibwemowin mainly was a language for prayers, like Latin in the Catholic liturgy. I was unaware for many years that Ojibwemowin was spoken in Canada, Minnesota and Wisconsin, though by a dwindling number of people.

By the time I began to study the language, I was living in New Hampshire, so for the first few years I used language tapes.

I never learned more than a few polite phrases that way, but the sound of the language in the author Basil Johnson's calm and dignified Anishinabe voice sustained me through bouts of homesickness. I spoke basic Ojibwe in the isolation of my car traveling here and there on twisting New England roads. Back then, as now, I carried my tapes everywhere.

The language bit deep into my heart, but it was an unfulfilled longing. I had nobody to speak it with, nobody who remembered my grandfather's standing with his sacred pipe in the woods next to a box elder tree, talking to the spirits. Not until I moved back to the Midwest and settled in Minneapolis did I find a fellow Ojibweg to learn with, and a teacher.

Mille Lacs's Ojibwe elder Jim Clark—Naawi-giizis, or Center of the Day—is a magnetically pleasant, sunny, crewcut World War II veteran with a mysterious kindliness that shows in his slightest gesture. When he laughs, everything about him laughs; and when he is serious, his eyes round like a boy's.

Naawi-giizis introduced me to the deep intelligence of the language and forever set me on a quest to speak it for one reason: I want to get the jokes. I also want to understand the prayers and the *adisookaanug*, the sacred stories, but the irresistible part of language for me is the explosion of hilarity that attends every other minute of an Ojibwe visit. As most speakers are now bilingual, the language is spiked with puns on both English and Ojibwe, most playing on the oddness of *gichi-mookomaan*, that is, big knife or American, habits and behavior.

This desire to deepen my alternate language puts me in an odd relationship to my first love, English. It is, after all, the language stuffed into my mother's ancestors' mouths. English is the reason she didn't speak her native language and the reason I can barely limp along in mine. English is an all-devouring language that has moved across North America like the fabulous plagues of locusts that darkened the sky and devoured even the handles of rakes and hoes. Yet the omnivorous nature of a colonial language is a writer's gift. Raised in the English language, I partake of a mongrel feast.

A hundred years ago most Ojibwe people spoke Ojibwemowin, but the Bureau of Indian Affairs and religious boarding schools punished and humiliated children who spoke native languages. The program worked, and there are now almost no fluent speakers of Ojibwe in the United States under the age of thirty. Speakers like Naawi-giizis value the language partly because it has been physically beaten out of so many people. Fluent speakers have had to fight for the language with their own flesh, have endured ridicule, have resisted shame and stubbornly pledged themselves to keep on talking the talk.

My relationship is of course very different. How do you go back to a language you never had? Why should a writer who loves her first language find it necessary and essential to complicate her life with another? Simple reasons, personal and impersonal. In the past few years I've found that I can talk of God only in this language, that somehow my grandfather's use of the language penetrated. The sound comforts me.

What the Ojibwe call the *Gizhe Manidoo*, the great and kind spirit residing in all that lives, what the Lakota call the Great Mystery, is associated for me with the flow of Ojibwemowin. My Catholic training touched me intellectually and symbolically but apparently never engaged my heart.

There is also this: Ojibwemowin is one of the few surviving languages that evolved to the present here in North America. The intelligence of this language is adapted as no other to the philosophy bound up in northern lands, lakes, rivers, forests, arid plains; to the animals and their particular habits; to the shades of meaning in the very placement of stones. As a North American writer it is essential to me that I try to understand our human relationship to place in the deepest way possible, using my favorite tool, language.

There are place names in Ojibwe and Dakota for every physical feature of Minnesota, including recent additions like city parks and dredged lakes. Ojibwemowin is not static, not confined to describing the world of some out-of-reach and sacred past. There are words for e-mail, computers, Internet, fax. For exotic animals in zoos. *Anaamibiig gookoosh*, the underwater pig, is a hippopotamus. *Nandookomeshiinh*, the lice hunter, is the monkey.

There are words for the serenity prayer used in 12-step programs and translations of nursery rhymes. The varieties of people other than Ojibwe or Anishinabe are also named: *Aiibiishaabookewininiwag*, the tea people, are Asians. *Agongosininiwag*, the chipmunk people, are Scandinavians. I'm still trying to find out why.

For years I saw only the surface of Ojibwemowin. With any study at all one looks deep into a stunning complex of verbs. Ojibwemowin is a language of verbs. All action. Two-thirds of the words are verbs, and for each verb there are as many as six thousand forms. The storm of verb forms makes it a wildly adaptive and powerfully precise language. *Changite-ige* describes the way a duck tips itself up in the water butt first. There is a word for what would happen if a man fell off a motorcycle with a pipe in his mouth and the stem of it went through the back of his head. There can be a verb for anything.

When it comes to nouns, there is some relief. There aren't many objects. With a modest if inadvertent political correctness, there are no designations of gender in Ojibwemowin. There are no feminine or masculine possessives or articles.

Nouns are mainly designated as alive or dead, animate or inanimate. The word for stone, *asin*, is animate. Stones are called grandfathers and grandmothers and are extremely important in Ojibwe philosophy. Once I began to think of stones as animate, I started to wonder whether I was picking up a stone or it was putting itself into my hand. Stones are not the same as they were to me in English. I can't write about a stone without considering it in Ojibwe and acknowledging that the Anishinabe universe began with a conversation between stones.

Ojibwemowin is also a language of emotions; shades of feeling can be mixed like paints. There is a word for what occurs when your heart is silently shedding tears. Ojibwe is especially good at describing intellectual states and the fine points of moral responsibility.

Ozozamenimaa pertains to a misuse of one's talents getting out of control. *Ozozamichige* implies you can still set things right. There are many more kinds of love than there are in English. There are myriad shades of emotional meaning to designate various family and clan members. It is a language that also recognizes the humanity of a creaturely

God, and the absurd and wondrous sexuality of even the most deeply religious beings.

Slowly the language has crept into my writing, replacing a word here, a concept there, beginning to carry weight. I've thought of course of writing stories in Ojibwe, like a reverse Nabokov. With my Ojibwe at the level of a dreamy four-year-old child's, I probably won't.

Though it was not originally a written language, people simply adapted the English alphabet and wrote phonetically. During the Second World War, Naawi-giizis wrote Ojibwe letters to his uncle from Europe. He spoke freely about his movements, as no censor could understand his writing. Ojibwe orthography has recently been standardized. Even so, it is an all-day task for me to write even one paragraph using verbs in their correct arcane form. And even then, there are so many dialects of Ojibwe that, for many speakers, I'll still have gotten it wrong.

As awful as my own Ojibwe must sound to a fluent speaker, I have never, ever, been greeted with a moment of impatience or laughter. Perhaps people wait until I've left the room. But more likely, I think, there is an urgency about attempting to speak the language. To Ojibwe speakers the language is a deeply loved entity. There is a spirit or an originating genius belonging to each word.

Before attempting to speak this language, a learner must acknowledge these spirits with gifts of tobacco and food. Anyone who attempts Ojibwemowin is engaged in something more than learning tongue twisters. However awkward my nouns, unstable my verbs, however stumbling my delivery, to engage in the language is to engage the spirit. Perhaps that is what my teachers know, and what my English will forgive.

Instant Novels?
In Your Dreams!

Thomas Fleming

Half awake in the dawn, I knew I was in a bedroom in Berlin. In the bed an attractive young German woman was having a bad dream. She tossed and turned and uttered anguished cries. Suddenly I was in the dream. A U-boat with a knight's head on the conning tower was cruising through the Atlantic's gray depths. Around it exploded a half-dozen depth charges. The boat tilted on its side and began to sink.

Now I—and the woman—were inside the boat, watching the drowning men gasp for a last breath as the water rose around them. We swam through the chaos until we reached the control room, where the captain, the woman's husband, awaited death with stoic defiance.

Then we were outside the U-boat again. Out of the depths swam a gigantic angel, as large as the boat, with huge staring eyes and a fixed hieratic smile. This incredible creature embraced the dying boat in its immense arms. Back in the

Berlin bedroom the woman awoke and thought: "The Path. The angel is part of the Path."

I awoke in my bedroom on East Seventy-second Street in Manhattan and raced to my computer. In an hour I had written the first chapter of my 1994 novel, *Loyalties*. In succeeding years I've puzzled more than once about where this vision came from. It utterly defies rational analysis. I was not thinking about writing a novel about the German resistance to Hitler, which is what the book became. I had only the dimmest knowledge about these tragic patriots, gleaned from reading Anthony Cave Brown's *Bodyguard of Lies* two or three years earlier. Why did it erupt in my imagination?

I had a similar experience with my 1992 novel, *Over There*. This was a book I had planned to write for years. It was going to be about my father, who had been promoted from sergeant to lieutenant during the battle of the Argonne. "Teddy Fleming as the immortal sergeant" was the way I summed it up.

Instead, one morning I awoke with a vision of a drunken white colonel driving a car down a highway outside San Antonio at suicidal speed. Beside him sat a frowning black sergeant. The colonel had a name: Malvern Hill Bliss. He was the son of a Maryland Confederate who had lost a leg in the Civil War battle of Malvern Hill. He was a Catholic whose wife and son had recently been killed by a Moro guerrilla in Mindinao. He was driving to a brothel where (I knew) Gen. John J. Pershing would interrupt Bliss's drunken amours to tell him that President Wilson had made Pershing head of the American Expeditionary Force and that he was taking Bliss to Europe with him to command a division.

In this whirling kaleidoscope Teddy Fleming as the

immortal sergeant virtually vanished. In the final version of the novel he had little more than a walk-on part. This outburst of imagination was almost as mysterious as the birth of *Loyalties*. But I could at least glimpse what my imagination was telling me. In most histories and novels, World War I seemed to be the triumph of death over life. My imagination was urging me to write a different book.

Pershing was taking Bliss to Europe with him because he, too, had been wounded by death, the soldier's enemy. He had lost his wife and three children fifteen months before, in a fire in their San Francisco quarters. He was summoning Bliss, the one man who understood what he felt, to help him confront death's terrific challenge, as well as the awesome task of rescuing the French and British from the brink of collapse and defeat. In a landscape of death *Over There* became a life-affirming book.

Such experiences have convinced me that Cushing Strout, the Cornell critic, knows whereof he speaks in his brilliant book *The Veracious Imagination*. He argues that the imagination is not simply a mental device that "makes things up." On the contrary, it is an intellectual tool, closely wedded to the writer's intelligence. What it chooses to imagine for a novel is integrally connected to the essence of what the writer, consciously or unconsciously, wants to say about the subject.

The visionary flash that gave birth to my 1987 novel, *Time and Tide*, illustrates this insight. I had been in the Navy during World War II and for twenty-five years had tried to write a novel about my experience. But I could never devise a satisfactory plot. One evening I was researching the battle of Savo Island for an article. This 1942 clash off

Guadalcanal was a dolorous American defeat. The conduct of the heavy cruiser USS *Chicago* was baffling. She had sailed away from the Japanese enemy after taking a single hit. After the battle, in which four other cruisers were sunk, the *Chicago*'s captain was relieved in disgrace.

In a swirling moment I suddenly saw the story that had eluded me for so long. The cruiser's captain, flamboyant, career-driven Winfield Kemble, would be relieved by his modest, low-keyed Annapolis roommate and best friend, Arthur McKay, who has orders to find out what happened off Savo that night and to make Kemble the scapegoat for the defeat. The imaginary ship would be the USS *Jefferson City*, a fitting name for the metaphor of American society that I hoped to make her.

The two captains would sum up the clash of ambition and integrity and friendship that often rolls American military men and their wives at the higher levels of command and also affects boardrooms and executive suites in peacetime America.

Sometimes a novel emerges simply as a voice, saying something that sounds almost silly at first. In the late '60s I spent four years writing a history of the United States Military Academy at West Point. I met many officers' wives and found them fascinating. They saw the Army experience in ways dramatically different from their husbands. For the next few years I heard a voice whispering:

The officers wives
The officers' wives
That's what we'll be
For the rest of our lives.

It didn't make much sense. Ten years later the entire novel—the three very different women who were main characters, their husbands, their children—surfaced, fully developed, ready to write. The song was sung at a party in the first chapter.

Liberty Tavern, my 1975 novel set in Revolutionary New Jersey, had an even stranger genesis. I saw a man making a toast: "Here's to all those that we love. Here's to all them that love us."

A crowded room responds: "Here's to all them that love those that love them. Love those that love them that love us!" These words turned out to be the last lines of the novel. They were the key to the main character, Jonathan Gifford, the ex-British officer who dominates the book.

My latest novel, *Hours of Gladness*, emerged as a single word: Mick. Then it became Mick O'Day. The name kept pushing against my consciousness. Slowly the character appeared: an Irish-American spiritually wounded by Vietnam, living with his fellow Irish-Americans in a New Jersey shore town, with the Vietnamese woman he loved now a refugee living nearby, untouchable, alienated forever.

Don't ask me how or why these things happen in my head. I only hope my brand of Mr. Strout's veracious imagination keeps working. At the moment another voice is whispering, "My three beauties." It has something to do with my father and his two hell-raising brothers. So far that's all I know. But I suspect there's more to come.

Goofing Off While the Muse Recharges

~

Richard Ford

Sometime in the middle of June I sat down to a ritual that, as much as any other, has typified my writing life: At the end of a very lengthy period during which I did basically nothing whatsoever of any good to man or beast, I got back to work. That is, I started writing again.

I don't mean to make this event seem momentous. There was no drum roll. The sound track was not the theme from *Rocky*. There was no sound track, just the quiet, scarcely noticeable shiftings in a man's daily protocols from one set of digital, inward habits to another.

No more solitary morning TV, no more taking my breakfast out, no more reflexive telephone communiques; instead, just the usual soup of things that continually wash through my brain suddenly beginning to need sorting out for use in a story. It was a bit like Army recruits who instantly become soldiers just by standing in a line wearing their street clothes. And as with the recruits, my re-enlistment to writing was accompanied by an unwelcome feeling of purpose.

Stopping and then starting up again is of course what all writers do. It's what any of us does: Finish this, pause, turn to that. Over time this repetition is one of those markers that cause us to say we are this, not that: EMS attendant, lawyer, car thief, cellist: novelist.

More than for most of my writer colleagues, this ritual—cease in order to resume—has always seemed to me to be an aesthetic, possibly even a moral postulate. Many of my acquaintances, however, simply can't wait to get on with writing, as if nature also abhors a motionless pencil.

One friend (until I barked at him) regularly called me at about cocktail hour simply to say, "Did you write today?" Others seem to eye the horizon line anxiously from the deep interior of whatever they're doing at the moment, trying, I suppose, to catch a flickering glimpse of what they might plunge into next. To them the stop preceding the start, the interval, is at best a needless blink in a life devoted to constant gazing. At worst, it provokes a worry, even a fear.

"I'm not writing," a close friend in Montana told me recently. "It's so depressing. I just wander around the house without knowing what to do. The world seems so drab."

I advised: "Try turning on the TV. That always works for me. I forget all about writing the second *SportsCenter* comes on."

And I mean it. In these thirty years I have made a strict point to take lavish periods away from writing, so much time that my writing life sometimes seems to involve not writing more than writing, a fact I warmly approve of.

Admittedly, over this time I've only written seven books, and about these seven there has yet arisen no unanimous critical huzzah. And undoubtedly some smarty-pants will argue that if I'd only written more, been more obsessed, driven myself harder, ground my molars lower and paused less, I'd be a better writer than I am.

But I never imagined I was in this business to break the writers' land speed record, or to put up big numbers (except, I've hoped, big numbers of readers). In any case, if I had written more and stopped less, not only would I have driven myself completely crazy, but almost certainly I would have proved even less good at writing stories than I am. Anyway, it's my business what I do. There are finally some things about ourselves that we know best.

Most writers write too much. Some writers write way too much, gauged by the quality of their accumulated oeuvre. I've never thought of myself as a man driven to write. I simply choose to do it, often when I can't be persuaded to do anything else; or when a dank feeling of uselessness comes over me, and I'm at a loss and have some time on my hands, such as when the World Series is over.

I would argue that only in this state of galvanic repose am I prepared to address the big subjects great literature requires: the affinities between bliss and bale, etc. Call it my version of inspiration, although it's entirely possible that my reliance on this protocol still causes even me to write too much. It's hard to write just enough.

Clearly, many writers write for reasons other than a desire to produce great literature for others' benefit. They write for therapy. They write (queasily) to "express" themselves. They write to give organization to, or to escape from, their long, long days. They write for money, or because they are obsessive. They write as a shout for help, or as an act of familial revenge. La, la, la. There are a lot of reasons to write a lot. Sometimes it works out OK.

Maybe my seemingly lax attitude comes from having had

working-class parents who slaved so that I could have a better life than they did—wouldn't have to work as hard—and my life is just a tribute to their success. But whatever the reason—piddling around doing something else, like driving from New Jersey to Memphis and then to Maine just to buy a used car, which I did last month—life comes well before writing to me; whereas writing, at least doing an awful lot of it, feels too much like hard work. I know my mother and father would give me their full support in this.

Not, I hasten to say, that writing is ever all that hard. Beware of writers who tell you how hard they work. (Beware of anybody who tries to tell you that.) Writing is indeed often dark and lonely, but no one really has to do it.

Yes, writing can be complicated, exhausting, isolating, abstracting, boring, dulling, briefly exhilarating; it can be made to be grueling and demoralizing. And occasionally it can produce rewards. But it's never as hard as, say, piloting an L-1011 into O'Hare on a snowy night in January, or doing brain surgery when you have to stand up for ten hours straight, and once you start you can't just stop. If you're a writer, you can stop anywhere, any time, and no one will care or ever know. Plus, the results might be better if you do.

For me the benefits of taking time off between big writing projects—novels, let's say—seem both manifest and manifold. For one thing, you get to put lived life first. V. S. Pritchett once wrote that a writer is a person observing life from across a frontier. Art after all (even writing) is always subordinate to life, always following it along. And life—that multifarious, multidimensional, collisional freight train of thoughts and sensations you experience away from your desk, when you walk down Fifty-sixth Street or drive to

Memphis—can be quite bracing (if you can just stand it) as well as useful for filling up the "well of unconscious cerebration" that Henry James thought contributed to the writer's ability actually to connect bliss and bale.

Time frittered away can also just seem like a nice reward for the grueling work you finished. Sometimes it's the only reward you get.

Most writers' work habits date from the days when they were beginners, and at some base level one's habits always involve a system of naive appraisal. You proceed in ways that let you figure out if what you're doing is acceptable to yourself.

Stopping and starting during any one day's writing invites you to judge what you just wrote. And enjoying a long interval between weighty endeavors invites such useful reassessments as: Do I have anything important left to add to the store of available reality? (Kurt Vonnegut decided he didn't.) Do I still wish to do this kind of work? Was the last thing I wrote really worth a hill of beans? Is there not something better I could be doing to make a significant mark on civilization's slate? Does anybody read what I write?

I mean, aren't such inquiries always interesting as well as being merely fearsome? Isn't there a measure of coldly cleansing exhilaration involved in appraising one's personal imperatives as though they were moral matters? Isn't that, as much as anything, why we became writers in the first place?

My view of the writers I admire is not that they are sturdy professionals equipped with a specific set of skills and how-tos, clear steps for career advancement and a saving ethical code; but rather that they are gamblers who practice a sort of fervidly demanding amateurism, whereby one completed, headlong endeavor doesn't teach the next one very much. And in the case of writing novels, one endeavor consumes almost entirely its own resources and generally leaves its author emptied, dazed and bewildered with a ringing in his ears.

Therefore a good spendthrift interval lasting a couple of seasons if not more, or at least until you can no longer stand to read the headlines of the newspaper, much less the articles that follow, can help to freshen the self, to reconfigure the new, while decommissioning worn-out preoccupations, habits, old stylistic tics—in essence help to "forget" everything in order that you "invent" something better. And by doing all this, we pay reverence to art's sacred incentive—that the whole self, the complete will, be engaged.

Finally, what seems hard about writing may not be what you think. For me what are testing are the requirements of writing that make a sustained and repeated acquaintance with the world an absolute necessity; that is, that I be convinced that nothing in the world outside the book is as interesting as what I'm doing inside the book that day. What's more demanding is to believe in my own contrivances and to think that unknown others with time on their hands will also be persuaded. To do that, it helps a lot to know what bright allures lie just outside your room and beyond the pale of your illusion.

A Novelist Breaches the
Border to Nonfiction

Gail Godwin

I said no immediately. An editor had just phoned John, my agent, with an idea: a book about the heart, the different ways we've imagined the heart through time and what those images tell us about the human condition. The editor wanted "a lush, writerly treatment with a narrative arc," John said.

I'd love to read a book like that, I said, but I can't do it; I'm a fiction writer. But the topic had snagged my imagination. I offered some suggestions: The book should have this, this and this in it. It shouldn't be a plodding survey. More of a broad, inclusive excursion in the company of an informed guide who has planned the route but left openings for surprises.

"It should be written from the writer's heart, whoever you get to write it," I told John.

Before I got off the phone with John, I had more or less described the book I was not going to write. "Let me sleep on it," I said.

Never bother to say you'll sleep on anything. In the first

place, you won't sleep; and in the second place, you've already agreed in your heart to do whatever you were supposed to sleep on.

My old reliable *Handbook to Literature* defines fiction as "narrative writing drawn from the imagination of the author rather than from history or fact," though it includes historical fiction, fictional biography, autobiographical history and the roman à clef. There is no entry for nonfiction, but *The Random House Dictionary* (1987) defines nonfiction as "narrative prose dealing with or offering opinions or conjectures upon facts and reality." The term came into general use through the cataloging of books as recently as 1905.

The first difference I experienced in crossing over from fiction to nonfiction was the publisher's willingness to draw up a contract on the basis of a scant proposal and tentative outline. As a fiction writer, I had been used to showing anywhere from fifty to two hundred polished pages of a novel in progress, though later in the game, when I had five or six novels behind me, I could say, "My new novel is tentatively titled ———, and it is going to be about ———," and the rider to the "satisfactory manuscript" clause would then specify only that the finished novel should "conform to the professional and literary standards" of certain (named) previous novels of mine.

If I had been an established nonfiction writer proposing my first novel, would it have been more of a risk to sign up a "work of imagination" than a work "based on facts and reality"? Where do you draw the line between the two kinds of prose?

During the writing of *Heart* I kept finding that such a line was elusive. The level of imagination can be very high in a work of nonfiction. Take the opening lines of Henry Adam's "travel book" and spiritual autobiography, *Mont Saint Michel and Chartres*: "The Archangel loved heights. Standing on the summit of the tower that crowned his church, wings upspread, sword uplifted, the devil crawling beneath."

Doesn't it read like the beginning of a fantasy or an allegory? We're inside the Archangel's head. But no, Adams is describing the tower of an actual church.

Conversely, what manner of prose animal does this opening sentence herald? "In February 1948, Communist leader Kiement Gottwald stepped out on the balcony of a Baroque palace in Prague."

A history of Czechoslovakia? A biography of Gottwald? No, a novel by Milan Kundera: his own distinctive mixture of fairy tale, political tract and autobiography, *The Book of Laughter and Forgetting*.

Though shelved separately in libraries and bookstores, *Mont Saint Michel and Chartres* and *The Book of Laughter and Forgetting* are both complex, personal works of intense imagination.

Maybe whether something is called fiction or nonfiction becomes arbitrary when you don't have to classify books. That doesn't mean that my experience of writing nonfiction wasn't different. It was, though not in ways I would have predicted.

I like to discuss my work in progress with people. I've never worried that my inspiration would evaporate from exposure; it's more likely to dry up under my withering self-scrutiny. These exchanges with others often shed light on where I'm going. But always before when I was discussing a novel in progress, my listener observed a certain decorum. They would comment when something in my plan excited them ("Your unreliable mentor gives me the shivers") or wonder how I would overcome a technical problem, but they respectfully hung back from suggesting content.

Not so with *Heart*. Everyone had something I must put in. "I'll send you my material about the heart in Egyptian afterlife," announced a friend as we took a walk. "I got fascinated when we lived in Cairo."

My exercise teacher said: "Be sure and put in Chinese medicine. It's full of wonderful heart concepts."

During the writing of *Heart* I learned that when you're drawing from history or shared cultural experiences and not just from your private stash, people feel entitled, perhaps duty bound, to supply material.

The most surprising difference was that the nonfiction book turned out to require less research than my novels. When I packed away my two years' worth of research for *Evensong*, the papers filled two empty Champagne cases. There were several pounds of data on military prisons in World War II, photocopied out-of-print books on millennium phenomena, microfilmed theses on orphanages in America, hefty rubber-banded clumps of material on firefighting, lung damage, bell-tower designs and the ordination process for priests. I had also acquired a sizable theological library. Whereas my two years' worth of research folders for *Heart* won't fill a single Champagne carton, and the books I needed to buy for the project were few.

I already owned most of the books needed for a meditation on the heart: the philosophers and psychologists, the artists and poets, the various religious texts (though I had to buy the Upanishads and a Koran), mythologies, world histories, symbol books, novels and poetry, lives of saints and mystics. And I knew where in them to look for what I needed: Ellie Dunn's lament in Shaw's *Heartbreak House*,

Portia's similar one in Bowen's *Death of the Heart*; the sort of connections that had been made from years of reading and were simply waiting to be organized and articulated.

I realized that in writing fiction I overcompensate on research because I am making up a whole world and have to convince myself I know where everything is and how characters got to be the way they are, even if I don't end up putting it in the novel. When Brother Tony finally spilled his story in *Evensong*, I didn't use much of my prison research, but all I'd read had helped me imagine prison as Tony would have experienced it. I could put in the odd detail that gave an authentic flavor to his travails.

As for the actual writing of *Heart*, by which I mean the mechanics of putting one word after another, of straining after the insight that flits by with gnatlike evasiveness, of clenching the mind to force from a clump of recalcitrant brain cells a word I knew perfectly well yesterday—how was that process different? It wasn't any different, that part of it, my personal style of word choice and arrangement.

My author's voice informs every page I produce, whether the subject is a fictional woman recalling in first person how she asked a man to cut her hair so he would propose marriage to her, or a cultural musing on how the ancient Egyptian proscription against "eating one's heart" (being angry) might elucidate our popular malediction to "eat your heart out." A page of mine will never be mistaken for a page of Jane Austen or Elmore Leonard or Margaret Atwood, however much I admire and relish their voices.

What I did discover, however, when I sat down to write my first full-length nonfiction work, was that a new inner critic materialized out of the shadows with her own set of no-nos. She blew on my heart instincts with her dry-ice breath and often smothered my creative joy. I have an old working relationship with my fiction-writing inner critic, a picky, prissy, buttoned-up man with a smile that is both sinister and obsequious. (Once, when he was being exasperating, I drew his portrait.) His job consists mostly of wringing his hands and being fearful that I'll fail at being marvelous. I've learned to coexist with him over the years, but she was something new.

She cast herself in the form of a beautiful, icy woman in a sari, the ghost figure of a professor I had in graduate school, who once beseeched me in her elegant Oxbridge accent to write a "real" thesis, not one of those "creative ones," even though the doctoral program at Iowa allowed it. I did not take her advice, the English department accepted my first published novel as my thesis, but for years afterward I kept my Ph.D. diploma unframed and mildewing in a drawer because I felt it was not quite authentic. And the kind of writing that would have made it authentic was exactly what my new inner critic kept insisting on, now that I was finally doing a real project.

In some ways I profited from her manifestation. When you are writing a work "based on facts and reality," you must be accountable. You must cite your sources. You may not filch from other people's translations without giving credit. But on the negative side, she kept squelching me: "Leave yourself out of this, Gail. You may report what the ancient Egyptians meant by 'eating one's heart' (being sure to cite Sir Wallis Budge as your source), and you may allow yourself to contrast and compare it with our contemporary imprecation. You may write in your own author's voice, since it's the only one you've got, but keep your personal experiences out of it."

She prevailed to the extent that when I turned in what I thought was the finished manuscript, the editor respectfully sent back twelve single-spaced pages of suggestions, almost all of which had to do with putting more of myself into the book. ("Could you tell us explicitly how this myth relates to your own personal understanding of the heart?" "Is there any personal or contemporary story you associate with this material?" "Can you be more open-hearted here?")

And so I took two more months and put more of myself into *Heart: A Personal Journey Through Its Myths and Meanings*. What kind of prose animal is it now? I won't venture to classify. I'd be quite happy to let it stand as a "complex, personal work of intense imagination."

Putting Pen to Paper, but Not Just Any Pen or Just Any Paper

Mary Gordon

There may be some writers who contemplate a day's work without dread, but I don't know them. Beckett had, tacked to the wall beside his desk, a card on which were written the words: "Fail. Fail again. Fail better."

It's a bad business, this writing. No marks on paper can ever measure up to the word's music in the mind, to the purity of the image before its ambush by language. Most of us awake paraphrasing words from the Book of Common Prayer, horrified by what we have done, what we have left undone, convinced that there is no health in us. We accomplish what we do, creating a series of stratagems to explode the horror. Mine involves notebooks and pens. I write by hand.

Some of my friends say that my handwriting is illegible, but they are wrong. I love my handwriting. I have no trouble reading it. Well, there was the time I misread *incite* for *create*. But that kind of thing hardly ever happens.

W. H. Auden says that everyone secretly loves his own handwriting the way everyone secretly loves the smell of his own . . . He used a term that cannot be employed in these pages. Who of us brought up before the progressive '60s can forget the thrill of the Palmer method, the up strokes and down strokes, the loops and curlicues. Mastering "script" was an entry into the real, adult world. It harnessed two primitive instincts: the desires to make marks and to communicate thoughts.

Writing by hand is laborious, and that is why typewriters were invented. But I believe that the labor has virtue, because of its very physicality. For one thing it involves flesh, blood and the thingness of pen and paper, those anchors that remind us that, however thoroughly we lose ourselves in the vortex of our invention, we inhabit a corporeal world.

I know that I talk about my pens and notebooks the way the master of a seraglio talked about his love slaves. But let me tell you about my notebooks and my pens.

My pen. It is a Waterman's, black enamel with a trim of gold. When I write with it, I feel as if I'm wearing a perfectly tailored suit, and my hair is flawlessly pulled back into a chignon. Elizabeth Bowen, maybe, only French. Anna de Noialles, but played by Deborah Kerr. My pen is elegant, even if I'm wearing the terry robe whose frayed state suggests a fashion statement from a gulag. My ink is Waterman's black. Once while traveling I could only find blue-black. I used it for a few weeks, but it made me feel like a punitive headmistress.

I bought my pen at Arthur Brown & Brother on West Forty-sixth Street in Manhattan. Oh, it was difficult. I could have chosen silver or malachite or tortoiseshell; I could have gone modern with banana yellow; I could have bought something used before, a "genuine antique." I could have chosen straw thin or cigar stubby. I had to decide about points: fine, medium, thick. Medium was modest, self-effacing, a "don't worry, be happy" partner. Thick asserted its authority and mine. But I chose fine; there was something about its resistance, the hint of a scratch, the brief reluctance to move on to the next thing that provided the taste of austerity and discretion I seemed (although I had not known it till that moment) to be after.

In my closet there is a shelf entirely devoted to notebooks. I choose among them for the perfect relationship between container and the thing contained. In choosing the notebooks, I am engaged not only in a process of categorization and differentiation, but in a geographical remembrance. I buy notebooks wherever I go in the world. Just as each country has a different cuisine, each has a different notebook culture. And friends who know my fetish bring me notebooks from their travels.

I have three types from France. One, given to me by a student whom I had introduced to Proust, is robin's-egg blue on the outside; written in formal-looking script are the words *livre de brouillon*, book of rough drafts. Its pages are unlined. In it I keep my thoughts on my daily reading of Proust.

The French specialize in soft-covered smallish notebooks; on my last trip to Paris I bought student exercise books in royal blue from the enormous Gilbert Jeune on Boulevard St.-Michel: their covers proclaim that I am a *conquerante*. In Orleans I bought notebooks of confectionary colors: lime, strawberry, lemon. *Calligraphie*, their black letters proclaim. These malleable darlings are best for travel writing or short stories.

In a smoke shop near Trinity College, Dublin, I bought long notebooks in canary (long fiction, not novels) and square red ones (journalism). Both the red and yellow have the outline of a tower on the front, and the word *Tara* in Celtic script. Across from the British Museum I found hard notebooks covered in a burlaplike material in turquoise, maroon and orange (literary criticism).

On my last trip to Italy I was contemplating a novel in three voices. So I bought three each of three kinds of notebooks; some, in a Tuscan candy store, covered in shiny licorice black; some terra-cotta, like the roofs I saw from my window. I bought those in a stationery store near the Pantheon on the same street where I bought a pair of forest-green suede gloves with a raspberry trim. Near Santa Maria in Trastevere I bought three ecclesiastical-looking notebooks covered in black cardboard with a red binding.

There are some that are so pretty I use them as a consolation for the nauseating work of revision: soft pastels, sky blue, powder pink, with a gray Art Deco design. I found them on a stand across from San Lorenzo in Florence, where I'd just come from seeing Michelangelo's allegorical sculptures in the Medici chapel, those masterpieces of lassitude or melancholy, those idols of inactivity and repose.

A secret of notebook lore is the treasure trove of Swedish notebooks, primary colors with neutral borders; fuchsia and mauve, peacock and dove-colored. These seem so healthy, so sturdy, that I use them for my most uncensored journals: they can take it; they will keep it to themselves; nothing can hurt them and mum's the word.

On a trip to Vermont I splurged on a book of handmade

paper bound in teal-colored suede. These are for sentences that I write for their beauty as sentences: one sentence only per handmade page.

So what do I do after I've played with my pen and notebooks like a time-killing kindergartner? Before I take pen to paper, I read. I can't begin my day reading fiction; I need the more intimate tone of letters and journals. From these journals and letters—the horse's mouth—I copy something that has taken my fancy, some exemplum or casual observation I take as advice. These usually go into the Swedish journal, except for the occasional sentence that shimmers on its own, and then it goes into the handmade Vermonter.

I move to Proust; three pages read in English, the same three in French. In my Proust notebook I write down whatever it is I've made of those dense and demanding sentences. Then I turn to my journal, where I feel free to write whatever narcissistic nonsense comes into my head.

I listen to music, often string quartets or piano sonatas. Tina Turner will come later in the day; when I'm at my desk, I need my soul calmed. I enjoy the music and the rhythm of the mindless copying. Or not entirely mindless; I'm luxuriating in the movement of the words which are, blessedly, not mine. I'm taking pleasure in the slow and rapid movements of my pen, leaving its black marks on the whiteness of the paper.

Then I proceed to the fiction I'm reading seriously, the one I'm using as a kind of tuning fork, the one I need to sound the tone I will take up in the fiction I'm writing at the time. I can't listen to music when reading poetry or fiction. Into the notebook I am using for the fiction I'm writing, I copy paragraphs whose heft and cadence I can learn from. And some days, if I'm lucky, the very movement of my hand, like a kind of dance, starts up another movement that allows me to forget the vanity, the folly, of what I am really about.

It is remarkably pleasant, before the failure starts, to use one's hand and wrist, to hold and savor pleasant objects, for the purpose of copying in one's own delightful penmanship the marks of those who have gone before. Those whom we cannot believe have ever thought of failing, or of (as I do each morning) envying hod carriers, toxic waste inspectors, any of those practitioners of high and graceful callings that involve jobs it is possible to do.

I don't know what people who work on computers do to get themselves started. I hope never to learn firsthand.

To See Your Story Clearly, Start by Pulling the Wool over Your Own Eyes

~

Kent Haruf

The habits and methods of writers are sometimes peculiar enough to be interesting.

John Cheever wrote some of his early stories in his underwear. Hemingway is said to have written some of his fiction while standing up. Thomas Wolfe reportedly wrote parts of his voluminous novels while leaning over the top of a refrigerator. Flannery O'Connor sat for two hours every day at a typewriter facing the back of a clothes dresser, so that in those last painful years, when she was dying of lupus, she'd have as close to nothing as possible to look at while she wrote her stories about sin.

Eudora Welty has said that she straight-pinned pieces of her stories together on the dining room table, as though she were pinning together parts of a dress. Maya Angelou secreted herself in a hotel room for days and weeks of concentrated isolation while she worked on her autobiographical tales. Richard Russo wrote his first novels in the secluded corners of cafés. As for me, I prefer a coal room in the basement of our house in southern Illinois, and I write my first drafts blind on an old manual typewriter.

When we bought the house six years ago, my wife and I swept out the coal room, put in a table and shelves and laid down a piece of carpet. The room is about six feet by nine and has a single ground-level window through which coal once was shoveled. Hanging from a nail above my desk is the skull of a Hereford bull, complete with horns and dark gaping eye sockets. The skull came from Cherry County, Nebraska, which is beautiful big grassy sandhill country; and if you shake the skull, you can still produce a sprinkling of sand from its calcified insides. I keep this skull hanging over my desk both for itself and because I want to think it prevents me from writing baloney.

I have a plat on the wall of the county in northeastern Colorado that is the prototype for the invented Holt County that I write about and where all of my invented people live and die and commit their acts of sudden kindness and unexpected cruelty. I have brown wrapping paper taped up on the wall, on which I make notes about whatever novel I'm working on, and I have several pictures on the wall drawn by my youngest daughter, who's an artist, and also four photographs of western landscape paintings by Keith Jacobshagen and Ben Darling, and—not least—I have on the wall a black-and-white photograph of a High Plains barbed-wire fence choked with tumbleweeds.

On my desk I keep a sapling chewed by a beaver. I also keep on my desk a bird's nest, a piece of black turf from Northern Ireland, a plastic bag of red sand from the stage at the new Globe Theatre (taken after the production of Shakespeare's *Winter's Tale*), a piece of brick and some paddock dirt from Faulkner's home at Rowan Oaks, an old-fashioned hand warmer in a velvet sack, a blue bandana, a jackknife that once belonged to my maternal grandfather, Roy Shaver, who was a sheep rancher in South Dakota, and an obsidian arrowhead my father found in the North Dakota Badlands, where he was born almost one hundred years ago.

I do not pay much attention to these things, but having them there makes a difference. I suppose it is in some way totemic. The things on my desk and on the walls above it connect me emotionally to memories, ways of living, people and geographical areas that are important to me. It's an emotional attachment to all these things that connects me up with the impulse to write. I don't feel sentimental about these things in any sloppy way, but I do feel a strong emotion remembering things, remembering people, remembering places and sights. Every time I go down to work, I feel as if I'm descending into a sacred place.

As for the work, once I get to my office, it's done in a ritualistic, habitual way. First of all, I admit that I have a special attachment to the old pulpy yellow paper that was once used by newspaper reporters. You can't buy it anymore. Or at least I can't. But I was very lucky about seven years ago when the secretary at the university where I'd been teaching discovered six reams of it while cleaning out old cabinets, and she gave them to me. It was a great gift to me, like manna, like a propitious omen.

I'm very frugal with this old yellow paper: I type on both sides. I believe I have enough to last me the rest of my writing career. I use it only for first drafts of the scenes in novels. And then I use a manual typewriter, a Royal, with a wide carriage, and write the first draft of a scene on this yellow paper and, as I say, I write the first draft blindly.

This is not new with me. It's the old notion of blinding

yourself so you can see. So you can see differently, I mean. I remove my glasses, pull a stocking cap down over my eyes, and type the first draft single-spaced on the yellow paper in the actual and metaphorical darkness behind my closed eyes, trying to avoid being distracted by syntax or diction or punctuation or grammar or spelling or word choice or anything else that would block the immediate delivery of the story.

I write an entire scene or section on one side of one page, in a very concentrated and incomplete way. I'm trying to avoid allowing the analytical part of my mind into the process too soon. Instead, I'm trying to stay in touch with subliminal, subconscious impulses and to get the story down in some spontaneous way.

I haven't always written in this peculiar manner. Formerly, like anyone else would, I wrote on a manual typewriter on yellow paper (which was still available twenty-five years ago) with my eyes wide open. I wrote my first novel, *The Tie That Binds*, in this way. Then computers became affordable, and I wrote my second novel, *Where You Once Belonged*, on a computer, but I never did like the way that felt.

I missed the tactile sensation of working with paper, the visceral rightness of it and the familiar clacking of typewriter keys. Also, it was too easy to rewrite each sentence on a computer, and I tend to rewrite endlessly, anyway. Furthermore, unless you print out constantly, you lose parts of drafts, certain phrases and sentences, that you may wish later you had saved. So when I began to write *Plainsong*, my third novel, I knew I wanted to go back to using a typewriter, at least for the first draft, and I knew I had to find a way to curb my tendency to rewrite each sentence so often that no sentence ever sounded good enough. That's when the notion of writing blind occurred to me.

It helps that I'm a decent typist. (I took a full year of typing in high school; I was the only male student in the second semester, a circumstance that was not altogether unpleasant.) Only once have I typed past the bottom of the page onto the platen, and I took that mistake as a healthy reminder to be concise. And there was only one time in my blindness that I got off the home row of my typewriter and wrote nonsense. That served as a healthy corrective, too. It's not hard to write nonsense, not much harder than it is to write slack prose.

After finishing the first draft, I work for as long as it takes (for two or three weeks, most often) to rework that first draft on a computer. Usually that involves expansion: filling in and adding to, but trying not to lose the spontaneous, direct sound. I use that first draft as a touchstone to make sure everything else in that section has the same sound, the same tone and impression of spontaneity. I revise until I feel I'm done, and then I am done with that section or scene. I don't often go back and change much after that. So when I finish the last chapter, having redrafted the last page sufficiently, I'm done with the book.

But it's important to me to maintain this impression of spontaneity. By spontaneity I mean a sense of freshness and vividness. Perhaps at times even a suggestion of awkwardness. Otherwise, to me prose sounds stilted and too polished, as if the life of it were perfected out of it. It's very difficult to arrive at this sense of freshness and spontaneity in prose—in my experience, it takes a great deal of effort and practice and years of concentrated apprenticeship—but I believe it is one of the most important attributes to achieve. That, and simplicity. And clarity. Those would be the holy trinity in the art of fiction writing.

Still, I have to say, writing is all messier and more a matter of dead ends and fits and starts than a recitation like this one makes it out to be. And perhaps because writing fiction—this weird practice of telling artful lies, this peculiar habit of inventing imaginary people who talk and move and sleep and dream and wake up and kick and kiss one another—is so bizarre in itself is the reason why writers have to find bizarre ways to make it possible even to consider doing it.

So of course they have to write in their underwear and face the backs of dressers. Of course they have to pull stocking caps down over their faces. Otherwise they might as well do something practical and ordinary, become doctors and lawyers and ditch diggers like everyone else.

Real Life, That Bizarre and Brazen Plagiarist

~

Carl Hiaasen

One time I had to kill this guy.

It was in a novel, but that didn't make it easy. My books are supposed to be funny, so even death should be carried out with a twist of wit. The pressure is wicked.

The bad guy in question, Pedro by name, was a sadistic security guard at a low-budget amusement park in the Florida Keys. Pedro was so addicted to anabolic steroids that he hooked himself to a rolling intravenous rig, which he dragged behind him on his rounds.

Two-thirds of the way through the novel, which was called *Native Tongue*, I decided it was time to get rid of Pedro—he was growing nastier by the page and, worse, beginning to distract from the heroics of my protagonist. So Pedro had to go. But how to do the deed?

Shooting him would be simple enough; overdosing him, tidy and quick. But I feared that readers wouldn't be satisfied. Heck, I wouldn't be satisfied. That's how detestable Pedro was: his demise had to be something special.

In the end I did what satirists throughout the ages have done: I poached from current events and embellished to suit my plot.

At the time I was doing the book, a peculiar controversy was brewing about captive bottlenose dolphins in Florida, where I live. Local theme parks had begun charging tourists $50 or more to frolic in the tanks with the sleek, acrobatic sea mammals.

Some of the dolphins, it turned out, had their own ideas of fun. They greeted the splashy human intruders with what marine biologists discreetly termed "high-risk activity." Often that activity was aggressively sexual, leaving the tourists with a truly unforgettable vacation experience.

I had written of this phenomenon in my day job as a columnist for the *Miami Herald.* Like so many true Florida stories, this one had been worth clipping for future reference.

It proved bad news for Pedro, my fictional villain. As luck would have it, the sleazy amusement park in my novel featured a rogue, untrainable cousin of Flipper.

How could I resist? A dark night, a frantic struggle on the catwalk, the dope-addled thug tumbles into the tank and . . . is promptly romanced to death by Dickie the Dolphin.

So that's how I bumped off the evil security guard. Readers seemed to agree that justice was well served, though many of them thought I made up the bit about the randy cetacean.

(I didn't. For proof, see "Quantitative Behavioral Study of Bottlenose Dolphins in Swim-With-the Dolphins Programs in the United States," published in the October 1995 issue of *Marine Mammal Science.*)

Every writer scrounges for inspiration in different places,

and there's no shame in raiding the headlines. It's necessary, in fact, when attempting contemporary satire. Sharp-edged humor relies on topical reference points.

Unfortunately for novelists, real life is getting way too funny and far-fetched. It's especially true in Miami, where the daily news seems to be scripted by David Lynch. Fact is routinely more fantastic than fiction.

Consider the fellow who was found with an adult alligator in his bed, and numerous tooth-sized wounds on his torso. Over the punctured man's protests, game wardens whisked the befuddled reptile to safety.

Naturally a lawsuit and protracted custody battle followed. After two years an appellate court finally decided in favor of the gator and against his smitten captor. Although I've saved the newspaper clipping ("Court: Gators in bed is bad idea"), I doubt I'll ever use the story in a novel. It cannot be improved upon.

These days writers of satire must be exceptionally choosy about their material, and their targets. Even then, true life is inclined to trump you.

Once I wrote a book called *Strip Tease*, in which a United States congressman becomes droolingly infatuated with an exotic dancer. The premise had been inspired partly by my own congressman, J. Herbert Burke, who was arrested in 1978 for behaving badly at a topless club in Fort Lauderdale.

In real life Burke, a Republican, simply had gotten drunk and grabby with the dancers. In the novel my fictional congressman, a Democrat, is deranged with lust. (The movie role was given to Burt Reynolds, a choice that surely would have delighted the late and not-so-dashing Burke.)

One night in 1996, shortly before the film version of *Strip Tease* was released, a man named Kendall B. Coffey purchased a $900 bottle of Champagne and led a dancer to a private salon in a South Dade adult club called Lipstik.

The dancer, whose stage name was Tiffany, said Coffey drank too much bubbly and, after a struggle, chomped down on her arm. The incident wouldn't have made the news but for the fact that Coffey was the United States attorney for the Southern District of Florida, one of the nation's most powerful prosecutors. He made no secret of his importance as bouncers firmly escorted him from the strip joint.

Kendall Coffey declined to discuss what had happened but abruptly resigned as United States attorney and went into private practice. The dancer went on national television to display the bite marks. Later her husband called to see if I wanted to write a book about her shocking experience.

I told him I already had. It wasn't the first time I felt plagiarized by real life, and it isn't likely to be the last.

Some novelists say they envy those of us who live in South Florida because our source material is so wondrously weird. True enough, but the toll on our imaginations is draining. On many days fiction seems like a futile mission.

Pilfering from the news is no longer enough; now we must compete with it. A prime example is the strange saga of little Elián González, which rips off elements of Tom Wolfe, Kurt Vonnegut, even Gabriel García Márquez.

A young Cuban boy sets off for the United States in a small boat with his mother and other refugees. The boat sinks, his mother perishes, and the child is found adrift: protected, relatives would later claim, by friendly (but not overly friendly) dolphins.

The boy is embraced by Miami's exile community as a sort of anti-Castro messiah, graced by mystical apparitions of the Virgin Mary and even Diane Sawyer, standing on her head. Meanwhile back in Havana the child is hailed as a lost soldier of the Revolution, a mini–Che Guevara beaming at the throngs from T-shirts and highway billboards.

Elián's father wants him back in Cuba. The relatives in Miami won't let him go. Demonstrators surround the house and vow to block any attempt to retrieve the child, though he is accepting visits from Gloria Estefan, Andy Garcia and other celebrities. As the tense city sleeps, the boy is snatched by federal agents and flown to his father. The next day from the Miami camp: "Second Elián theory . . ."

I can't tell you how often I get asked if Elián will turn up in my next book. The challenge is too daunting, and not because the real-life drama defies satire. It is satire.

Just look who's railing at the press conference: one of the dozen high-priced lawyers hired to prevent Elián's father from regaining custody. Why, it's none other than Kendall B. Coffey, the aforementioned ex–United States attorney and alleged stripper biter!

How deliciously twisted and surreal.

Once it might have made a grand scene in a funny novel, but not now. It's too true to be good.

Sustained by Fiction
While Facing
Life's Facts

~

Alice Hoffman

I was told I had cancer on a beautiful blue day in July. I was out on Cape Cod, finishing the first draft of a novel when the telephone rang. I had thought it was about time for me to have a bit of good luck, and when I heard my surgeon's voice I assumed I was safe. In novels people were called into offices for bad news, and anyway, it was far too gorgeous a day for tragedy. Roses were in full bloom. Bees rumbled by the windowpanes, lazy with pollen and heat.

I was certain my doctor was phoning to tell me the biopsy had come back negative, I was absolutely sure of it, but then she said, "Alice, I'm sorry." I could hear the concern and sadness in her voice, and I understood that some things are true no matter how and when you're told. In a single moment, the world as I knew it dropped away from me, leaving me on a far and distant planet, one where there was no gravity and no oxygen and nothing made sense anymore.

It had been a bad few years for my family. My beloved

sister-in-law Jo Ann had lost a courageous battle with brain cancer; my mother had suffered a severe stroke, then had been diagnosed with breast cancer. I had spent two years completely involved in the health care of several people I loved, finishing up my novel *Here on Earth* during hours stolen so early in the morning that the birds were still asleep. By the time *Here on Earth* was chosen as an Oprah Book Club book, I myself was not feeling well. Two days after I returned from Chicago, I reached down and felt a lump in my breast.

All through my sister-in-law Jo Ann's illness I had been writing short stories. I needed a fictional place to which I could escape and had neither the time nor the psychic energy for a larger project. But these were a novelist's stories, and they quickly became interwoven, the tale of a family deep in the trenches of the same sort of struggle my family now faced.

I was at the hospital every day for months, and the world outside, those people with plans—the lovers, the new parents, the students—seemed far less real than the fictional world I was creating. When Jo Ann asked me to find her a grave site, a heartbreaking mission if ever there was one, my characters from "Local Girls" made a similar trek on the very same day, although they were far wiser than I, and far more optimistic. Frankly, I don't know if I could have made it through that particular afternoon without the assistance of the women from "Local Girls."

In my experience, ill people become more themselves, as if once the excess was stripped away only the truest core of themselves remained. In my sister-in-law Jo Ann's case, she became sweeter with each day, a kinder and more compassionate person despite her agony. My mother, always one to embrace life, was set to see *Eyes Wide Shut* with her eighteen-year-old grandson on the day she died. My other sister-in-law, Maryellen, diagnosed with breast cancer a few weeks after I was, used her own medical background to become an amazing researcher, as knowledgeable as any expert.

And who was I at the very bottom of my soul, beneath skin and blood and bones? I was not as kindhearted and gracious as Jo Ann, not as fearless as my mother, not as capable and independent as Maryellen. I knew who I was when I put my surgery off, a foolish thing to do, and yet I felt compelled to finish the first draft of my new novel. In a time when everything around me seemed completely out of control, when lives were being cut short and fate seemed especially cruel, I had the need to get to an ending of something. I was desperate to know how things turned out, in fiction if not in life. More than ever, more than anything, I was a writer.

I removed myself from everyone but my closest friends and family. I told almost no one about my illness, and instead turned to what I had always found most healing. Writers don't choose their craft; they need to write in order to face the world, and this was still true for me. Even now, writing was a transcendent experience. When I became too ill to sit up for long, I moved a futon into my office and went from desk to bed, back and forth until the line between dreaming and writing was nothing more than a thin, translucent thread.

What was real and what was imagined became braided together. I lived in my own world and the world of my book simultaneously. I could lie on a table during a bone scan and yet slip into the river where water lilies floated downstream, feet sinking into the soft mud. I could be walking through snowstorms, moonlight, fields of roses while receiving radiation.

An insightful, experienced oncologist told me that cancer need not be a person's whole book, only a chapter. Still, novelists know that some chapters inform all others. These are the chapters of your life that wallop you and teach you and bring you to tears, that invite you to step to the other side of the curtain, the one that divides those of us who must face our destiny sooner rather than later. What I was looking for during ten months of chemotherapy and radiation was a way to make sense of sorrow and loss.

I wrote to find beauty and purpose, to know that love is possible and lasting and real, to see daylilies and swimming pools, loyalty and devotion, even though my eyes were closed and all that surrounded me was a darkened room. I wrote because that was who I was at the core, and if I was too damaged to walk around the block, I was lucky all the same. Once I got to my desk, once I started writing, I still believed anything was possible.

The Enduring Commitment of a Faithful Storyteller

~

Maureen Howard

Not long ago I came upon a copy of the first and only story I ever published. It did not appear to be absolutely dreadful, but then I read only the first page. I have not written a story since. The novel became my game.

When I wrote that story, I was not unserious about becoming a writer, though I hadn't a notion of what, over the years, that might entail. Looking back, I cannot disown that shallow girl who presumed she had an entry into a phantom world of letters. Now I might ask her: What were you getting yourself into?

Writing fiction is not about first love, that blush of self-love when you discover your name in print. It's about passion and endurance, a combination of desire and grunt work often at odds with each other. More like a long marriage? Yes, the rekindling of the love of writing and a commitment to the solitary hours finding the word, tone, style—and may I mention the meaning?—why you are telling this story that will become a book with its pages.

This vocation, let's not call it a profession, has come to be about witnessing my time, personal and public time that are joined at the breast, inextricable. My education began in the Silent '50s, a misnomer like so many tags pinned on an era. We had our say, somewhat too politely, when Senator McCarthy came to deliver his incoherent ramblings at my women's college.

Modernism was in high regard in the classroom. With reverence I read Virginia Woolf, memorized long passages of Eliot's *Waste Land*, thrilled to the order of Pound's "Make it new" and the bold grammar of Gertrude Stein while writing wry undergraduate stories in imitation of sophisticated *New Yorker* fare. And in those years, the not-so-dowdy '50s, great American writers—Melville, Hawthorne, Poe and Emily Dickinson—were taken out of their glass bookcases, read with fresh attention by a new breed of scholars, many of them paying off their debt to the GI Bill.

Yes, the '50s were a feast for an earnest student who believed literature should be awarded its capital *L.* Of course the modernist's manifestos and the works that I held dear were radical more than forty years earlier, if we go by Woolf's famous pronouncement, "On or about December 1910 human character changed."

The battle against the poetic eloquence of Victorian versification and the soothing moral views of the Edwardian novel was long over, yet the aims of modernism declared before World War I were congenial to the years that followed World War II. Man's dislocation in an uncaring urban landscape dovetailed nicely enough with the loss of self we read in Eisenhower's prophecy of a "military-industrial complex."

The reward of looking back must be the ability to move

on, otherwise I must count myself a period piece, like the ancient beauty I see on my block with the pompadour, bright lipstick and ankle bracelet of her day. And moving on I understood that the venerated works of my modern masters and mistresses were not the only act in town. There followed, in panoramic succession, the irreverent canticles of the '60s, the liberating discovery of suppressed women's voices, the playtime of postmodernism with its fair field (or cage) of irony, the subdued mumble of minimalism and the literature of inclusion, let us hope here for the long run.

In this swift take on my forty—can that be right?—forty years of writing, I see myself as stationary yet moving. It's rather like standing on one of those conveyer belts in an airport. Eventually the track deposits the traveler, and only I can know my destination: the silent workroom of the solo flight in which the dangerous adventure is to discover the center, the still point of a novel that must be of my time yet not be swept along by fashion. Failure is written into the script. Like Ginger and Fred in the pratfalls of their ice-skating routine, you pick yourself up, brush yourself off and start all over again.

I believe that's how I would tell it straight to that star-struck girl who spent her last dollar on train fare to New Haven to hear Eliot's somber recitation of "The Dry Salvages." Or it may have been Robert Frost, whose readings were somber, too. But in a collection of Eliot's essays I find a letter from someone named Gerald telling me to take the 11:15 train from Northampton, Massachusetts, to arrive on time at Dwight Chapel. I borrowed the money to return to college, perhaps from Gerald, but he is lost to history.

I admit to inventing female characters driven to lecture the young on the past, on history if you will, both public and private. Lecturing themselves, I'd say, in hopes that examining the time they have lived through may tell them where they are, perhaps even who they are. I'm instructing myself, for after all, I am my first and most unforgiving audience.

When did I first understand that handing the pages over to be printed and bound, to be read by an audience beyond the workroom, was an act of exposure? Oh, not in the manner of a pulpy tell-all memoir, but in the flagrant display of myself in the rhythm of a sentence, the shape of a paragraph, the coincidental turn of plot; in the very subject of the decline of gritty cities and fractured love chosen for a work of fiction.

For all the voices and masks of my performance, there is an intimacy with the reader. We are in this game together. Reading, real reading, is a strenuous and pleasurable contact sport. Fun, but it's not television. In *Art Objects* Jeanette Winterson calls reading sexy. I'll go along with that smart idea. Reading, I might say to my students, is not like dating; it's a matter of full engagement.

Moving on in time: what if, as a very bright student proposed last semester, what if you don't feel entitled to what was once considered serious, even heroic themes? What if you are fidgety, embarrassed, speaking of commitment, never mind art? What if, in the presence of mass media and vast systems, words fail? Then write to the market; there's nothing wrong with that. Forget the poor marginalized literary novel with its shameless dedication. But remember, even *Seinfeld* with so much ready wit and amusing disenchantment has closed up shop.

Look to the wonders and terrors that await us as the book faces up to technology. The scribes went under with the invention of movable type, but respect for language did not pass away. I now look to the cursor's beat as well as the legal pad begging me for the next sentence. Words: that's all I've got aside from a dollop of imagination, but only think what it will be for you who come after. Technology will elicit new forms, and you may be much like an itinerant story-teller of old on the Internet, or whatever they will call it. You may drop in to spin your yarn by any man's fire.

I may not be around to scold you, if you do not take care with words. In "Modern Fiction" Woolf imagined that if the art of fiction came alive, "she would undoubtedly bid us break her and bully her, as well as honor and love her, for so her youth is renewed and her sovereignty assured." There I go again, back to an idol of my schoolgirl '50s, to her essay of 1919.

As for me, I am writing about Audubon, the first time I have attempted a historical tale. He killed all those birds for the love of nature and science. Or for his art, I believe.

But one day he winged a red cockaded woodpecker and brought it live into his workroom. The bird went about his business pecking at the walls, while the artist drew its black plumage ringed with white stripes, its sharp bill and blue talons, the red feather in its cap. In *The Birds of America* three of these woodpeckers are perched on a pine branch, a bit of invention to portray his specimen in full dimension. In this way the naturalist's aims seem much like the task of a writer of fiction, to record the truth enhanced by fancy.

I am writing in this time when dimension is virtual, an easy yet marvelous manipulation of reality. But let me tell you the best part of the Audubon story: when he was finished with his work, he opened the window and let his subject go free.

Inventing Life Steals Time, Living Life Begs It Back

Gish Jen

Last year I almost quit writing. I almost quit even though I was working well, even though I remained fascinated by the process of writing—the endless surprise of the sentences, and the satisfaction of thoughts taking form. I had a new book I wanted to write, the book I am now writing, which I knew to be a good project. I knew, what's more, that I was not written out, something for which I have perhaps morbidly always watched: I have long vowed not to keep on past the point where I ought best stop.

I was not there yet. Still, I almost quit because I felt the writing life was not life, because I felt I was writing instead of living.

There is never enough time for writing; it is a parallel universe where the days, inconveniently, are also twenty-four hours long. Every moment spent in one's real life is a moment missed in one's writing life, and vice versa.

To write is to understand why Keats writes of living "under an everlasting restraint, never relieved except when

104

I am composing." It is to recognize Kafka's longing to be locked in the innermost room of a basement, with food anonymously left for him. It is to know why Alice Munro describes the face of the artist as unfriendly; and it is to envy Philip Roth, who, rumor has it, has sequestered himself in a cabin in the Berkshires. He is writing, writing, people say, writing without distractions, only writing. To which the news part of us asks: Is that a life? Can you really call that a life? That is our sanity speaking. But another part, the writer part, answers, yes. One must live in order to have something to write about. That's the commonplace wisdom, and to be engaged with the world is no bad thing; it is essential. Still the bulk of everyday life comes as an interruption. Some people maintain that everything becomes material, but in truth it does not. It is entirely possible, for starters, to have too much of one kind of material; ask anyone in a menial job. But this is the stuff of another essay.

Allow me to claim that at forty-five, a mother of young children, I have a life that is mostly not material, that I simply live. Writing competes with that life and shortens its run. I struggle not to hurry my time with my children; I endeavor to lose myself with them even as I squeeze every last minute out of the rest of the day. I calculate; I weigh; I optimize. That I may lose myself again in my work, I map out the day, the route, the menu. I duck, I duck. I hoard the hours and despair in traffic jams. Worse, I keep an eye on my involvements. I give myself freely enough to others, but only so freely. I wonder if writing is worth this last price in particular. Art is selfish, Cynthia Ozick has said. Lyndall Gordon has brought us face to face with the coldbloodedness of Henry James and T. S. Eliot; Ozick has deemed the work worth it. Faulkner proclaimed the writer's only responsibility to be to his art. He famously claimed that if he had to rob his mother, he would not hesitate, and that "the 'Ode on a Grecian Urn' is worth any number of old ladies."

We might wonder today if it is worth any number of young men; but let's not. For the central question is: Even if a certain ruthlessness were necessary and justified in the case of Henry James, say, would it be justified for the rest of us?

I know I will indeed quit writing before I put live humans on the altar; I am sorry enough to be short with people, sometimes, or intermittently available. But I do not know what is right. When people talk about being between worlds, they generally mean cultural dislocation of a geo-political sort. Writers, though, are also caught between worlds. We may profess clarity about our allegiance, but novelists particularly cannot escape a concern with the moral. In truth, the possessed—of any stripe probably—are as inwardly divided as the dispossessed.

My crisis was a crisis of faith. It is common enough in midlife to feel newly shadowed by death; perhaps it was no surprise that writing began to seem an ultimately futile exercise, a pitiful attempt to give our leafy lives rocklike weight and meaning. Increasingly I doubted writing's worth and, correspondingly, rued its cost.

I tried quitting, therefore, in various degrees for some months. I gardened, I lunched, I talked to leafleteers. I con-tributed to causes. I chatted with dog owners. I enjoyed my children—in the lingo of our time, I savored them. I modeled for them fearlessness before live crabs. I modeled openness to new sports.

Yet I found life without work strangely lifeless. I wish I could claim that I went back to work because I had an exceptional contribution to make to the world, or because I found the words to dress down Old Man Death; but in fact I went back because life without prose was prosaic. It seemed as though the wind had stopped blowing. It seemed as though someone had disinvented music—such silence. I felt as though I had lost one of my senses.

I did have fun not working. I liked feeling I had something to spare and—faddishly, perhaps—I liked feeling open to the here and now. But more and more my here and now encompassed an awareness of things missing.

I missed reasoning with history, I missed roaming a large world. I missed tangling with language. I missed the shoulder to the wall of work. I missed discovering what I thought—or rather, watching what I thought I thought dissolve under my pen. I missed looking hard at things. I missed stalking a plot. I missed being ridden by the imagination, not so much into the sunset as through it.

But most of all, I missed the orientation that came with experiencing myself as distinctly—exhilaratingly, uncomfortably—singular. (How firmly this frames the real world. With what live interest one stands, paradoxically, at the window.) Also I missed communing with mostly dead authors. Of course, I was still reading; but I felt as though I were at a party, sitting out the dance.

I walked past a reservoir in the spring and saw an ice island. This was gray-black and submerged enough that it could have been the reflection of a cloud, except that it was covered with birds. The birds were ankle deep in the cold water; pointing in all directions, they seemed, despite their concerted stares, to be scattered. The island was something I'd seen and admired every year, but when I looked at it this time, I saw that it was transitory yet permanent, that its islandness depended on the water, which would destroy it and create it again.

The water and the ice were antagonistic, but not only antagonistic. The water was of the ice, after all, and the ice of the water; the water gave rise to the ice. Their relationship was what James Alan McPherson might have called one of antagonistic cooperation.

I saw that reservoir, and walked around it again, and one day went back to work. I was working hard enough for a while that I forgot about the ice island. I was simply living, working, living, working, bothered by interruptions but trying not to be so bothered. I was, in short, back to trying to balance my work and life.

Then one day I had a chance to ask Grace Paley how she had balanced so many things. There is no balance, she said flatly. And though we were on a summer road in Oregon when she said that—a road whose asphalt smacked and stuck to our sneakers—I saw my spring reservoir, with its ice island melting, reappearing, melting, reappearing. How peaceful an image, and how heartening—I realized it had heartened me—to think the island inevitable, to think the system stable. Perhaps in real life it was. As a guiding metaphor, though, it was limited and misleading.

Next to the road where Paley and I walked there was a great Oregonian river—one first-class river, Paley called it—roaring, roaring, inexorable. You couldn't swim in that river, even in the summer. It was too fast and too cold, too primal, unforgiving, torrential, a continual implacable avalanche, oblivious to night and day. To distract us a little from its force, there were, charmingly, pools and rivulets of wildflowers. Also there were high dry mountains, green with improbably matchstick trees. It was a crime not to hike those mountains. I vowed to go for a hike the next day. I set my alarm and, in the morning, put on my boots, then braved my computer instead.

A mathematician friend recently explained that there is a whole class of mathematical statements that can be called independent. These are propositions that can neither be proved true nor be proved false—which fall outside the realm of mathematical certainty. I asked my friend if he found these distressing. He answered no, quite the contrary, he found them wonderful. Many people thought of mathematics as possessing a platonic perfection, he said, which they loved. And he loved what they loved—that wondrous order, etc. But also he loved the fact that at certain points mathematics failed. He said he loved it that there were discrepancies, things that could not be reconciled, and, listening, I nodded in an ache of gathering recognition.

Could I come, like my friend, to appreciate deep discrepancies? (Henry Green said life, after all, was one discrepancy after another.) Could I, too, come not only to accept but also to embrace the irreconcilable? Perhaps I could. Perhaps I had already. Perhaps, I thought, I would write about it.

Pesky Themes Will Emerge When You're Not Looking

Diane Johnson

I've been going around doing readings from a new novel (*Le Mariage*), and often, on these occasions, I've been asked surprising questions about its themes. At first I was somewhat confounded by this. The novelist may be the last to know the theme of her work, may even have avoided thinking about it too particularly, lest, like happiness, it disappear on too close examination or seem too thin and flimsy to live.

In Seattle a man asked me what the theme of rescued cats and dogs in my books meant. I had to think about that, because I hadn't really noticed they were there. Freud would say those cats and dogs are children, but that doesn't seem quite right to me.

Must a novel have a theme? If so, who is in charge of it?

You can't help but wonder if each writer has themes typical to him, if the themes are as particular to the writer as to the work. To read, as I have, of my own books, that they are full of desperate women fleeing their circumstances, greatly surprised this contented and settled housewife. Certainly I have never thought of them that way. To me, my heroines are interpretive consciousnesses through whom to observe external events, in Iran, California or France.

I have written elsewhere about the plight of the reliable female narrator, a modern innovation perhaps, for whom we are unprepared by a literary tradition of heroines who were only acted upon. My friend Max Byrd says that all fiction can be reduced to one of two plots: a stranger comes to town, or someone goes on a trip. And mine are the latter, that's all, about travelers to whom things happen, as things will.

But that's not all about them. Any novel has lots of themes, if I understand the word correctly. It seems like a holdover term from high school English class, useful for discussing novels, but not very relevant to the process of writing them. There's something too close to "thesis" about it; the idea of imposing a preconception is anathema to a novelist who likes to imagine she is observing life and manners without any didactic intention and without forcing her characters to follow a plan.

Of course a writer, like anybody, has a set of general ideas: the inhumanity of man to man, or that life is a struggle, or that nature is beautiful. Some of the ideas will be received ideas; some may be original or idiosyncratic or even suspect, as was said of Ayn Rand's, for instance, or some of T. S. Eliot's, or Pound's. Taken together, a writer's themes are thought to typify the writer despite him- or herself, except for protean geniuses like Shakespeare, invisible in the dense thicket of their contradictions.

I suppose the major theme of a given work is the sum of all its ideas. That's implicit in those joke contests on the

Internet about Merged Novels, in which people compress the essence of two books into one, like "The Maltese Faulkner." ("Is the black bird a tortured symbol of Sam's struggles with race and family? Or is it merely a crow, mocking his attempts to understand? Or is it worth a cool mil?") Or "Catch-22 in the Rye." ("Holden learns that if you're insane, you'll probably flunk out of prep school, but if you're flunking out of prep school, you're probably not insane.")

But every novel is a "spongy tract," as E. M. Forster put it, a tissue of ideas so dense and various it would be impossible to tease them all out.

Too many themes and the novelist risks committing a "novel of ideas," a term that can conceal a note of reservation. As a phrase, "novel of ideas" is gathered from what seems now a somewhat dated typology used to categorize all novels as "of ideas," or as comedy of manners, or action, romance and so on, depending on the general effect. These were also shorthand ways of saying serious, boring, comic, moving account of personal anguish, love story, etc.

Even while there is a liking for the glib identification of themes, there is a resistance to the idea of ideas in novels. Two examples from my own experience:

The British publisher of *Le Divorce*, a novel about a young woman's coming to worldliness in Paris, omitted an entire chapter wherein Americans in Paris in about 1995 fall into a bitter dispute about the Vietnam War, a subject still dividing us after thirty years. The publisher thought this would not be interesting to a British audience. Now people ask how I could have been so docile about allowing this omission, and the answer is, I don't know. Maybe I was still insecure about that theme.

Another time, a French translator, under the impression

that *Persian Nights*, a novel about the political situation in prerevolutionary Iran, was a bodice-ripper, a genre the French are fond of, omitted all the heroine's observations of the political scene and stressed all her moments of personal danger, preferably the risk of rape (which in fact never came up). Here I did protest, and the problem was partly fixed.

Several reviewers of Susan Sontag's new novel *In America* have used the expression "novel of ideas," perhaps because the characters have ideas about Fourier's utopianism, or methods of acting, and discuss them. But you have to wonder what a novel without ideas would be like. One idea or theme in, say, Forster's *A Passage to India* is that people from different cultures rarely understand one another. Reduced to this simple statement, *A Passage to India* has the same theme as many novels that many other writers, including me in *Le Mariage*, have tried to write.

In its particulars of course *A Passage to India* is utterly unlike any other novel. Is it a novel of ideas or a comedy of manners? The characters discuss philosophy. "When evil occurs, it expresses the whole of the universe," says the Indian professor Godbole. Asked if he means that good and evil are the same, he says: "Oh, no . . . good and evil are different, as their names imply. But, in my humble opinion, they are both of them aspects of my Lord." He is talking to Fielding, for whom good and evil seem expressions of the indifference of the universe. Where does Forster stand in this difference of opinion? Does he take a stand?

Can the novelist entirely control the ideas in her text, or conceal herself among them? There's the phenomenon well known to writers whose characters, given their head, take off and do or say things the writer did not foresee. The writing has a Ouija board will of its own.

On the other hand there are the covert operations of your own character—your personal obsessions, perhaps—that ordain that, however you start out, you end up with the sort of novel only you would write. (Obviously these two are functions of each other: the unexpected crops up out of some less conscious realm of your self.) There's age, birth order, geography. Nationality is certainly part of the imperatives of our natures, something that we can't help and that has programmed us.

Of course you yourself can change with the years, with the events life deals you. I feel myself constantly struggling against some imperative of my own nature that dictates that no matter how much I want to write a serious, moving psychological novel, I end up with the sort of comic or tragicomic novel I have seen referred to as "of manners," reflecting my interest—and it is true that I'm interested in manners—in the way people behave and especially the way people behave when out of their own culture, or how people in other cultures behave.

But novels are never about what they are about; that is, there is always deeper, or more general, significance. The author may not be aware of this till she is pretty far along with it. A novel's whole pattern is rarely apparent at the outset of writing, or even at the end; that is when the writer finds out what a novel is about, and the job becomes one of understanding and deepening or sharpening what is already written. That is finding the theme.

If the writer is the last to identify the theme, probably we as readers don't consciously articulate the theme as we read either. When we are asked what a book is about, we tend to focus on some element of the plot, to say, "It's about a woman who was or wasn't molested in a cave in India," or "an orphan who has to work as a governess in a wild, remote house."

We fasten on the principal feature of the action. But what we get out of a book is the lesson or the theme: courage, the indomitability of the human spirit in the case of *Jane Eyre* (and all the works of Charlotte Brontë) and in *A Passage to India* things about integrity and pride, especially on the part of the misfit. These deep messages are the satisfying qualities that make us admire a book.

If a book had a wicked or meretricious message, we might reject or mistrust it, or in some way feel it to be subversive. Or we might be taken in by it, briefly. History is full of "dangerous" books, though they never prevail. But attempts to suppress them always eventually backfire, too. The moral careers of books are always fascinating.

Sitting Down a Novelist, Getting Up a Playwright

～

Ward Just

I have never thought writing novels was hard work. Hard work was commercial fishing out of New Bedford or Gloucester or driving a sixteen-wheel truck. Novels have more to do with desire—translating desire into prose—and a temperament that accepts concentration over the long haul, meaning the ability to sit alone in one place day by day.

Writing novels bears some modest (very modest) comparison to grinding on the higher slopes of the PGA tour, magical afternoons bunkered by afternoons of routine or appalling play and reminding yourself every minute to trust your swing.

Middle-aged golfers watching the Houston Open on television last May turned their faces to the wall when the forty-six-year-old Craig Stadler, playing beautifully from tee to green, missed short putts on four consecutive play-off holes to lose the match to Robert Allenby, not yet thirty. Allenby was not playing well, except on the green, where it counted.

My heart went out to Stadler, gray-haired, red-faced, so weary and impatient, so eager to get it over with. During the four-day run of the tournament he had used up his ration of concentration. He needed a distraction, something droll or alarming, anything that would divide him from the task at hand and cause him to reflect. His five-foot putts had become a kind of tyranny. (And the five-foot putt is the golfer's equivalent of the true sentence that completes the chapter.)

I hoped for a monstrous rainstorm so Stadler could go away, get a good night's sleep and return the following morning. Meanwhile Allenby was as steady as a metronome, completing his chapters with the authority and—it has to be said—the slow motion of Henry James in his late period.

For many years I have tried to find an agreeable distraction, something more sideline than hobby, some avocation that was not too difficult or tyrannical or long-term. When the sentences began to fall apart, there would be this other thing to do, my equivalent of a good night's sleep: except the sleep might last for weeks. Of course there would be money in it, whatever it was.

I was willing to try almost anything. The truth is, I thought of this activity as a day at the racetrack. If you forgot about hunches, if you studied the form and bet every race, the odds were good that you would cash at least one ticket. Perhaps, if you were clever enough, a win ticket or even the daily double.

My children described this as Dad's search for a get-rich-quick scheme. But I only wanted to get out of the office.

For a long time I thought I could do voice-overs, the sort of thing that David McCullough does so well for *The*

American Experience. I have what I have always believed was a nicely modulated baritone, perhaps riddled a little around the edges by tobacco and scotch, but inviting nonetheless. That voice, I imagined people saying, that voice has been around. I asked a friend where I might take this undiscovered talent, and after listening to a tape, she said commercials. An arthritis remedy or something to do with heartburn or anxiety. McCullough is safe, she added.

And that brings me to Paris, February 1991. A long, gray winter, the dollar falling. My wife and I had moved from one overpriced apartment to another. I had completed the novel I was working on and was unwilling to begin another right away.

The worm of avocation had begun to crawl yet again, to no positive result. I spent my time watching the Persian Gulf War on television and visiting museums, never neglecting a nourishing meal at the end of the day. It was at one of these that two German friends, a diplomat and a historian, suggested we go together to see Patrick Suskind's play *La Contrebasse*, at the Theatre des Arts-Hebertot. The author was a friend of theirs.

I very much admired his novel *Perfume,* and under normal circumstances I would have agreed at once. It's always interesting when writers change hats: poets to novelists, novelists to playwrights. But circumstances were not normal. *La Contrebasse* was in French, and I did not speak French. My wife spoke French. She dealt with the plumbers, electricians, doctors, dentists and *Le Monde*. I was the one who sat in cafés and listened to conversations, inventing my own translations.

Don't worry, the diplomat said. We'll translate for you. The historian seconded the motion.

My wife insisted that I knew more French than I thought I did, and, *en tout cas*, everyone would chip in with key words and phrases.

What a pleasure for those sitting around us, I thought but did not say.

So we attended *La Contrebasse* by Patrick Suskind at the Theatre des Arts-Hebertot. It turned out to be a one-character play involving a musician and his double bass. I had matters pretty well in hand until about the fifth minute, when the narrative collapsed. I had no idea what the actor, Jacques Villeret, was saying.

I inferred that he and his double bass had an extremely complicated relationship, and that things were not going well between them. The action transpired in the musician's apartment somewhere in bohemian Paris, the Marais, perhaps, or Montparnasse.

The audience was laughing; my wife and our German friends were enthralled. So any idea of assistance with the salient words and phrases was forgotten. For me these were minutes of oceanic boredom until my mind suddenly slipped into another realm altogether. As I did in cafés, I began to supply my own translation. Just as suddenly, the musician and his double bass vanished. In their places appeared a newspaper reporter and his typewriter.

The newspaper reporter was middle-aged, as was the musician; and the typewriter was well worn and talismanic, as was the double bass. The reporter seemed to have an affectionate relationship with the machine; it was his career that was going to hell.

The set remained the same: a couch, a desk, two tables, chairs here and there, a bookcase. But Paris had become Cincinnati because in my mind's eye I saw the poster that hung on my office wall in the rue des Saints-Peres: Edward Hopper's *Street Scene, Gloucester*, Cincinnati Art Museum.

My newspaperman was fifty-five. He was a soloist, a little scornful of the ensemble. Along the way he managed to win a Pulitzer Prize, a badge he thought was not entirely deserved. When the curtain rose, Act I, Scene 1, he erupted on the stage in a fury, as Jacques Villeret had done.

I have no idea of the cause of the musician's agitation, but the newspaperman was returning from the funeral of a colleague, with the justified suspicion that his editor wanted to fire him. If my newsman had thought of himself as a musician, he would have chosen Bach, for the measured cadence and formality of expression. But since he thought of himself as an artist, he believed that on his best days he captured something of Hopper. His editor preferred Roy Lichtenstein, so my man was headed for the shelf.

How did it go? my wife asked when *La Contrebasse* was over.

Wonderful, I said.

She looked at me with astonishment.

You understood it?

Everything, I said. Nothing.

Lowell Limpett took four days to write. Really, all I had to do was transcribe what I had written in my head during the ninety-minute reverie in the Theatre des Arts-Hebertot. I had been given a free bet at the track, so the writing was a lark, as if I had decided to compose a long letter to a friend or a bedtime story for my grandchildren.

I put into it all I had ever known or heard about newspaper reporters reaching the end of their one-way street, all seen through the lens of my own newspaper experience of decades before; alternative histories, as someone called it.

My character was more restrained than Patrick Suskind's, at least as Jacques Villeret played him. But his double bass and my typewriter were brothers, and I can remember now the unfathomable rapid-fire French mutating into measured American idiom, and my surprise when the curtain fell and the audience broke into applause.

I wrote the play, had a good laugh and thought that I had found my sideline, except that I had no expectation that anyone would want to risk a production. So it was a pro bono sideline, with some vanity thrown in.

Lowell Limpett had its debut in Paris in March 1991: a living room full of invited guests; many, many drinks before the curtain rose; Alan Riding, a reporter for the *New York Times*, in the title role. Somewhere a videotape survives, but owing to inattention or too much Bordeaux or mechanical failure, the tape is without sound. Since virtually everyone in attendance was connected to the news business, there was high hilarity. Everyone thought it had commercial possibilities. What a vehicle! And so funny!

That summer I sent it around, first to friends in the theater business, then to friends of the friends, finally to theater companies. But you know this story. This is an old story without possibilities, because all unhappy theater stories are alike. Each happy theater story is happy in its own way. I put *Lowell Limpett* into the discard file and forgot about it, reminded only when I glanced at Hopper's picture on my office wall.

And there matters stood for eight years. We returned to New England. I published four novels, did a voice-over, continued my struggles with golf, searching always for an agreeable sideline.

A few months ago I got a call from the playwright

Michael Weller. He had seen the manuscript of *Lowell Limpett* in 1991 and liked it, and he now proposed that I sign up with the mentor program for emerging playwrights at the Cherry Lane Alternative Theater in Manhattan. You get a mentor to smooth the rough edges and the promise of a ten-day run at the Cherry Lane Alternative.

If I had any doubts—and what doubts were there to have?—they were forgotten when I learned the identity of my mentor. Wendy Wasserstein owns a Pulitzer Prize, just like Lowell Limpett. Unlike Lowell Limpett, she's young enough to be my daughter.

Mentee, she said, and began to cackle.

What can I expect? I asked.

This is a get-rich-quick scheme, she said, and laughed and laughed.

Those Words That Echo . . . Echo . . . Echo Through Life

~

Jamaica Kincaid

How do I write? Why do I write? What do I write? This is what I am writing: I am writing *Mr. Potter*. It begins in this way; this is its first sentence: "Mr. Potter was my father, my father's name was Mr. Potter." So much went into that one sentence; much happened before I settled on those eleven words.

Walking up and down in the little room in which I write, sitting down and then getting up out of the chair that is in the little room in which I write, I wanted to go to the bathroom. In the bathroom Mr. Potter vanished from my mind; I examined the tiles on the floor in front of me and found them ugly, worn out.

I looked at the faucet and the sink in front of me, but not too closely; I did not examine those. I flushed the toilet and I thought: Will the plumbing now just back up? Does the septic need pumping? Should I call Mr. A. Aaron? But Mr. A. Aaron's name is not that at all. His real name is something quite far from that. His real name is something like Mr.

Christian or Mr. Zenith, though I cannot remember exactly. He only calls himself A. Aaron so he can be the first listing in the telephone book under the heading "Septic Tanks & Systems—Cleaning." I come back and look at Mr. Potter.

"Mr. Potter," I write, and I put clothes on him, even though I do not see him naked, for he was my father, and just now he is not yet dead. He is a young man, and I am not yet born. Oh, I believe I am seeing him as a little boy; as a little boy he has clothes, but he has not shoes. I do not place him in shoes until he is—I have not decided when exactly I shall allow him to wear shoes.

And then after many days of this and that and back and forth, I wrote, with a certainty that I did not necessarily intend to last, "Mr. Potter was my father, my father's name was Mr. Potter." And Mr. Potter remained my father, and Mr. Potter remained my father's name for a long time, even up to now.

And then? I grew tired of that sentence and those eleven words just sitting there all alone followed by all that blank space. I grew sad at seeing that sentence and those eleven words just sitting there followed by nothing, nothing and nothing again. After many days it frightened me to see nothing but that one sentence and those eleven words and nothing, nothing and nothing again came after them. "Say something," I said to Mr. Potter. To myself I had nothing to say.

Speaking no longer to Mr. Potter, speaking no longer to myself in regard to Mr. Potter, I got up at five o'clock in the morning and at half-past five o'clock went running with my friend Meg and a man named Dennis Murray; he builds houses of every kind in the city of Bennington in the state of Vermont.

"My father is dead," I said to Dennis one morning as we were just past the Mahar funeral parlor on Main Street. I never make an effort to speak before the funeral parlor. I despise death and consider it a humiliation and in any case much overdone and so plan never to do it myself and plan never to have anything at all to do with it, for it is so contagious. I have noticed that when you know people who die, you catch it and end up dead, too.

"My father is dead," I said to Dennis, but he could not hear me for he was far ahead. He runs at a faster pace than I do, and he thought I was agreeing with something he had just said about the weekend he had just spent hiking into the woods and spending the night and fishing with a friend whose name I cannot remember and catching many trout and cooking them and eating them and going to sleep in a tent while there was a great downpour of rain outside and waking up the next morning and having the best pancakes and fishing again and doing everything again and all of it as perfect as it had been before and then coming home to his wife who loves him very much.

And the perfect narrative of Dennis's life, uninterrupted by any feelings of approaching and then leaving behind the Mahar funeral parlor, did not make me envious or make me grieve that Mr. Potter's life remained frozen in the vault that was his name and the vault of being only my father.

The days then rapidly grew thick into all darkness with only small spaces of light (that is autumn) and then remained solidly all darkness with only small patches of light (that is winter), and then the darkness slowly thinned out (that is spring), but the light was never as overwhelming in its way as the darkness was overwhelmingly dark in its way (that is summer). So, too, was the night dark except for when the moon was full and the day bright with light, except for when clouds blocked out the sun. And Mr. Potter remained my father, and my father's name remained Mr. Potter for a very long time.

One day when I seemed uncertain about which foot to put first, the one in front of the other, my husband said to me, "Mrs. S., Mrs. S., how are you doing?" And "Are you OK?" The first letter in his family's chosen name is S. Our children go to school every day on a great big bus that was painted yellow and driven by a woman named Verta. A man named Mr. Sweet came and picked up our rubbish.

In the American way we have much rubbish, and Mr. Sweet is hard of hearing. Saying to him, as I feel I must if I see him, I must say to him, "Hallo, Mr. Sweet." And since he cannot hear me, he is deaf, he looks at me and then holds his ear forward, cupping it in the palm of his hand, as if it were a receptacle, for he wants it to receive the sounds that I am making.

"What?" says Mr. Sweet. "Hallo," I say again, and Mr. Sweet is then very nice and sincerely so, and he asks if I could pay him for the eight weeks he has picked up the rubbish without being paid.

"But no," I say to him, and then I explain that I am not allowed to write checks because I never put the debits and balances in their proper columns, and I make a mess of the household accounts. Mr. Sweet says, "Yep, yep," and then Mr. Sweet says he will see me next week. Mr. Sweet does not know about Mr. Potter, not in the way of my writing about him, not in the way of Mr. Potter as a real person.

And one day, after all sorts of ups and downs and many travails that are interesting, especially to me, Mr. Potter was driving a motorcar and dressing in a way imitative of men who had enormous amounts of money. And of course Mr. Potter was right to imitate the wardrobe of men who had enormous amounts of money, for without the existence of Mr. Potter and people like him, working very hard and being paid a mere pittance, there can be no enormous amounts of money. And I am Mr. Potter's daughter, so I know this.

But that "and one day" left me bereft and exhausted and feeling empty; and that "and one day" is just what I want when in the process of encountering a certain aspect of my world.

And then that one day, that one day after Mr. Potter's life advanced and exploded on the page, I had to have my lunch, but I could not eat too much of anything, not even plain green leaves. I could only eat very small amounts of anything, for I wanted to fit into my nice blue (tilting to lavender) silk taffeta skirt, a skirt that has box pleats. And I so love my nice blue (tilting to lavender) silk taffeta skirt with the box pleats and will not eat too much of anything, even just plain green leaves, for I look very beautiful in it. I look most beautiful in it when I am in a room all by myself, just alone with only my reflection, no one at all there to observe me.

In the early afternoon, just after I have eaten my lunch, I look at Mr. Potter, in my own way, a way I am imagining, a way that is most certainly true and real. (His name really was Roderick Potter; he really was my father.) He cannot look back at me unless I make him do so, and I shall never make him do so.

The telephone rings, and I do not answer it. The telephone rings, and I do not answer it. The telephone rings, I answer it, and on the other end is someone employed by one of my many creditors asking me to satisfy my debt. I promise to do so in a given time, but I have no money. I like having no money. I do not like having no money. I only like to have contempt for people who have a great deal of money and are unhappy even so, or are happy with money in a way that I find contemptible.

Driving past a sign that says "Yield," driving past the house where a dentist lives, driving past the house where the chiropractor I see from time to time lives, swiftly I pass by a sloping moist field that in spring is filled up with marsh marigolds. Swiftly I go past the home for delinquent children. Swiftly I go to await my children getting off the bus with Verta.

My children will soon get off the school bus, the one painted a harsh yellow, and it is driven by Verta. "Mr. Shoul," I say to myself, for I am all alone in the car having driven so swiftly. "Mr. Shoul," I say, for I now can see that I have saddled Mr. Potter with this personality, Mr. Shoul. And Mr. Shoul is a merchant, an ordinary merchant, specializing in nothing particular; he sells anything. Mr. Shoul sells everything. Mr. Shoul might sell Mr. Potter; on the other hand he might draw the line at selling Mr. Potter. And I have saddled Mr. Potter with Mr. Shoul.

Mr. Potter does not know the world. He is produced by the world, but he is not familiar with the world. He does not know its parameters. Mr. Potter was my father, my father's name was Mr. Potter. My children pour out of the bus. My daughter (she is fourteen) hurls an insult at my son (he is ten). His small self (the self that is not seen) crumbles to the ground; I rush to pick up his self that is not seen but has fallen to the ground and bring it back together again with his self that I can see.

I look at her, my daughter. What should I do? For her

selves (one or two or three or more) are not all in one bundle, tied up together either.

"Mr. Shoul," I say to myself, for I am at the bus stop and can tell no one what I am really thinking. "Mr. Shoul," I say. What to tell Mr. Potter about Mr. Shoul, where to begin?

"Mr. Shoul!" I shout at Mr. Potter, but Mr. Potter cannot hear me. I have left him at home on the page, the white page, the clean white page, all alone with Mr. Shoul. "Mr. Shoul," I will write, "Mr. Shoul," I will tell Mr. Potter, "Mr. Shoul comes from Lebanon."

A Forbidden Territory
Familiar to All

Barbara Kingsolver

R eader, hear my confession: I'm writing an unchaste
   novel. It's a little shocking, even to me. In my previous
books I've mostly written about sex by means of the space
break. One reviewer claimed I'd written the shortest sex
scene in the English language. I know the scene he meant;
the action turns when one character notices a cellophane
crackle in the other's shirt pocket and declares that if he has
a condom in there, this is her lucky day. The scene then proceeds, in its entirety:

He did. It was. (Space break!)

I think my readers rely on me for a certain reserve, judg-
ing from the college course adoptions and the mothers who
say they've shared my books with their daughters. They may
be in for a surprise this time around. Not that the sex is gra-
tuitous, I keep telling myself. This novel is about life, in a
biological sense: the rules that connect, divide and govern
living species, including their tireless compunction to repro-
duce themselves.

In this tale the birds do it, the mushrooms do it, and the people do it, starting on page 6 already. I'm having a good old time writing about it, too. I've always felt I was getting away with something marginally legal, inventing fantasies for a living. But now it seems an outright scandal. I send my kids off to school in the morning, scuttle to my office, close the door, and hoo boy, *les bons temps roulent!*

Now that I'm closing in on a finished draft, though, I've begun to think about the people who will soon be sitting in their homes, on airplanes and in subways with their hands on this book. Many people. My mother, for instance.

My writer-friend Nancy, a practical New Englander, offered this counsel:

"Barbara, you're in your forties now, and you have two children. She knows that you know."

Yes, all right, she does. But what about the man from the Ag Extension Service, whom I've asked to vet my book's agricultural setting for accuracy? How do I hand this manuscript to him? And what about those English Lit teachers? I don't mind that they know I know, or that I think about it, in circumstances outside my own experience. Come on, who doesn't? Most people I know couldn't construct a good plot to save their souls, but can and do, I suspect, imagine detailed sexual scenarios complete with dialogue (if they're female) and a sense of place.

But they don't pass them around for others to read, for heaven's sake. My dread is that people will take my book for something other than literature and me for something other than a serious writer. In anxious moments I've begun combing my bookshelves for fellow offenders.

Yes, there are plenty of authors before me who have put explicitly sexual scenes into literature. There's a particularly lovely one in the center of David Guterson's *Snow Falling on Cedars*, there are sweetly funny ones in John Irving, and of course we have John Updike, Philip Roth and Henry Miller. (Notice the dearth of women on this list.) Even such distinguished eighteenth-century gents as Ben Franklin and Jonathan Swift scored the occasional love scene in their prose.

But I was surprised, on the humid afternoon I spent pulling down books and looking for scenes that had burned themselves into my memory, to see how often they were implied situations rather than step-by-step enactments. Copious use of the space break, in other words.

The scene in *Lady Chatterley's Lover* I've remembered down the years, it turns out, was mostly invented by me, not D. H. Lawrence. (And given Lawrence's knowledge of love from the female perspective, is that any wonder?) In actual word count, if the literary novels in my bookcase accurately represent human experience, it looks as if people spend roughly half their time in intelligent dialogue about the meaning of their lives, and 1 percent of it practicing or contemplating coition.

Excuse me, but I don't think so.

Why should literary authors shy away from something so important? Nobody else does. If we calibrated human experience on the basis of television, magazine covers and billboards, we would have to conclude that humans devote more time to copulation than to sleeping, eating and accessorizing the hot new summer look, combined. (Possibly even more than shooting one another with firearms, though that's a tough call.) Filmmakers don't risk being taken less seriously for including sexual content; in fact, they may risk it if they don't.

But serious literature seems to be looking the other way, ready to take on anything else, with impunity. Myself, I've written about every awful thing from the death of a child to the morality of political assassination, and I've never felt fainthearted before. What is it about describing acts of love that makes me go pale? There is, of course, the claim that women who make a public show of being acquainted with sexuality are expressing deviance, but that's also said about women who make a show of knowing anything, and I can't imagine being daunted by such nonsense.

For decent folk of any gender, the official and legal position of our culture is that sex takes place in private, and that's surely part of the problem. Private things—newfound love, family disagreements and spiritual faith, to name a few—can quickly become banal or irritating when moved into the public arena. But new love, family squabbles and spirituality are rich ground for literature when they're handled with care. Writers don't avoid them on grounds of privacy, but rather take it as duty to draw insights from personal things and render them universal. Nothing could be more secret, after all, than the inside of another person's mind, and that is just where a novel takes us, usually from page 1. No subject is too private for good fiction if it can be made beautiful and enlightening.

That may be the rub right there. Making it beautiful is no small trick. The language of coition has been stolen, or rather, I think, it has been divvied up like chips in a poker game among pornography, consumerism and the medical profession. None of these players are concerned with aesthetics, so the linguistic chips have become unpretty by association. *Vagina* is fatally paired with *speculum*. Any word you can name for the male sex organ or its, um, movement seems to be the property of Larry Flynt. Even a perfectly serviceable word like *nut*, when uttered by an adult, causes paroxysms in sixth-grade boys.

My word processing program's thesaurus has washed its hands of the matter: it eschews any word remotely associated with making love. *Coitus*, for example, claims to be NOT FOUND, and the program coyly suggests as the nearest alternative *coincide with?* It also pleads ignorant on *penis* and suggests *pen friend*. A writer in work-avoidance mode could amuse herself all day.

I realize linguistic aesthetics may not be Microsoft's concern here; more likely it's mothers. *Roget's* does much better, reinforcing my conviction that the book is mightier (or at least braver) than the computer. My St. Martin's *Roget's Thesaurus* obligingly offers up fifteen synonyms for coition—though some are dubious, like "couplement"—and an impressive twenty-eight descriptors for genitalia, though again some of these are obscure. In a scene where lingam meets yoni, I'm not even sure who I'm rooting for.

Nevertheless, the language is ours for the taking. Fiction writers have found elegant ways to describe life on other planets, or in a rabbit warren, or an elephant tribe, inventing the language they needed to navigate passages previously uncharted by our tongue. We don't normally call off the game on account of linguistic handicaps. When it comes to the couplement of yoni, I think the real handicap is a cultural one.

We live in a strange land where marketers can display teenage models in the receptive lordotic posture (look it up) to sell jeans or liquor, but the basics of human procreation can't be discussed in a middle-school science class without sparking parental ire. The same is true for evolution, incidentally, and I think the reason is the same: our tradition is to deny, for all we're worth, that we're in any way connected with the rest of life on earth. We don't come from it, we're not part of it, we own it.

It is deeply threatening to our ideology, at the corporate and theological levels, to admit we're constrained by the laws of biology. Sex is the ultimate animal necessity. We can't get rid of it. The harder we try to deny it official status, the more it asserts itself in banal, embarrassing ways. And so here we are, modern Americans with our heads soaked in frank sexual imagery and our feet planted in our Puritanical heritage, and any novelist with something to say about procreation or the lordotic posture has to negotiate that territory. Great sex is more rare in art than in life because it's harder to do.

To write about sex at all, we must first face down the polite pretense that it doesn't really matter to us and acknowledge that in the grand scheme of things, nothing could matter more. In the quiet of our writing rooms we have to corral the beast and find a way to tell of its terror and beauty. We must own up to its gravity. We also must accept an uncomfortable intimacy with our readers in the admission that, yes, we've both done this. We must warn our mothers before the book comes out. We must accept the economic reality that this one won't make the core English Lit curriculum.

Still, in spite of everything, I'm determined to write about the biological exigencies of human life, and where can I start the journey except through this mined harbor? It's a risk I'll have to take.

Reader, don't blush. I know you know.

Summoning the Mystery
and Tragedy, but in a
Subterranean Way

Hans Koning

I arrived in this country on a Dutch freighter that had taken a month to get me from Singapore to San Pedro, the port of Los Angeles. They had to unlock the turnstile at the San Pedro streetcar station for me, as it hadn't been constructed with passengers toting large suitcases in mind. That was in the winter of 1951. I had spent a year in Indonesia as a radio journalist, but I never thought of myself as anything but a serious novelist: my first novel was planned and ready in my head.

It was to be written in the first person, and the reader would learn about its protagonist only from his almost abstract thoughts about the human condition and his own life within it. That was my reaction against what I called to myself "the two fingers of whiskey school of writing," in which reality is supposed to be pinned to the pages by a most detailed spelling out of its manifestations, as when we learn that the hero filled his glass with two fingers of scotch, a splash of soda, one slice of lemon and two ice cubes.

(Different from most young writers I have since met, I didn't feel the slightest admiration for Ernest Hemingway.)

When I started writing the novel, I found of course that the purity of the concept needed considerable dilution if I did not want it to become just an exhausting gimmick. Nonetheless it took me years to get the novel published.

The second or third time of making the rounds, it ended up with Henry Robbins, then a junior editor at Alfred A. Knopf, and he took it. (Alfred had promised him autonomy and didn't stop him; but Alfred announced at his own sales conference that he hated the book.) That was *The Affair*, and it was very widely reviewed. I didn't realize this was unusual for a first novel.

Dutch was my mother tongue, but I had been in the British army and had started to think and dream in English. Dutch and English were close kin once. *The Canterbury Tales* often reads like Dutch. English has become marvelously richer of course, getting at its disposal not only the Germanic but also the Roman wellspring of words.

My English was all right then; even those Westchester ladies who at that time, working at home, were the free-lance and scholarly text editors for several New York publishing houses, found little to object. (I've often felt that starting out at the edge of the language, so to speak, was a blessing in disguise, because it gives you an awareness of words that is different from that of the native speaker, who, like Huckleberry Finn, may not think of, say, *glove* as one of the possible words for the thing but rather as the thing itself.)

But there was a perceived European-ness about my novel that I had put in on purpose, and that stayed with me through the twelve novels I've written since. It was perceived as European by some editors and reviewers, but I did not think of it that way at all. It was the idea that a novel should be committed, what they call in France *engagé*.

The very fact that in English it is expressed by that awkward word *committed* shows that it's a qualification that plays little role in the American writing scene. It means to me that if you want to write a serious novel, you should not only be out to entertain but you should also, in a hidden way, reflect on the world's justice and injustice, hope and illusion.

Trollope and Oscar Wilde agree with me here, not to mention Brecht or García Lorca, but the very idea makes many reviewers nervous. They think it makes a novel political, which in their vocabulary becomes synonymous with tendentious. Some editors, and of late agents (who now often occupy terrain where once editors feared to tread), tell me that it is bad for sales and that I'd do better to replace it with "a commercial core."

There is of course always the danger that all this committedness turns your novel into a lengthy pamphlet that bores, and then loses, your readers. But that danger is a challenge to your writing, not to the idea as such. In order for a novel to be engagé, it isn't in the least necessary that it deals with a momentous subject. It does not have to deal with war and peace, love and death. It may be about a lottery swindle in Brooklyn or a suburban academic whose sex life is a shambles.

What I believe it needs is evidence that its writer has gone through an awareness of the human condition, its comedy and melodrama, its mystery and tragedy. Isn't it that awareness that can give the crucial dimension to the most banal occurrences we may want to describe? It is not an awareness tied to a specific political ideology, and there is nothing specifically European about it, unless it be that so many American critics have expounded the thesis that "true art is above politics," which is to say—although they won't say it that way—that it is committed to the status quo.

No writer can float in a void above the battle; there are always links. There is a link between the potato famine and James Joyce's *Ulysses*. There is a link between the heroes and heroines of Henry James and the basics of their society; if they had to run off to nine-to-five jobs, they would have lost most of their literary interest. There is even a link between the portraits of Rembrandt and the plundering of the Indies by the Dutch East India Company. To be above politics (politics in the widest sense) doesn't seem meritorious to me. I believe one can only be that way through total indifference to our world, or appalling incomprehension.

When I used the term *serious writing*, I was not making a value judgment. I realize authors of nonserious novels achieve what they set out to achieve, and often with unsurpassed professionalism. Serious writing is not better; it has a different origin. It is writing that you have to write, what you hear in your mind.

You don't inquire what is selling those days. You don't worry about what editors or reviewers may like or not like. (That comes afterward.) You don't read chapters to friends or to a long-suffering husband or wife in order to get an independent judgment. Your own judgment is independent. You don't accept any suggested change except where you made a factual or grammatical mistake. My motto has been through all those years: Not a comma.

Please don't imagine that I think Jane Austen should really have introduced a battle of Napoleon or a strike of the

Lancashire weavers in her stories. She lived at a time when, in the words of Saint-Just, human happiness was invented, and she wrote of and for men and women who had just become aware of their own unique destinies, which is why we are still interested in the marriage prospects of her heroines. That cult of the individual was precisely the essence of her time, and thus she became more strongly engaged to it than if she had bothered with Napoleon. That is not what we are about now, however. Perhaps the essence of our time is that we have to learn to look beyond our own individual lives.

As for me, I keep aiming toward that novel that is just that, a true novel, but a novel for our time, dealing with an essential theme and an essential message in a subterranean, carefully hidden way, a message like a snake in the grass, as Trollope put it. There'll be no boy meets tractor, nor even a professor meets sophomore.

A reader (and a reviewer) should find just as much in it as he or she is prepared to accept. Until one night, perhaps, when such a reader, for instance of my *Kleber Flight*, cannot get to sleep, and then suddenly the snake would raise its head, and he or she would start wondering if there was, after all, sense to what its hero (or antihero) was about on his destructive flight in that little Piper Tomahawk airplane. Or so I hope.

Comforting Lessons in
Arranging Life's Details

~

David Leavitt

The other night I saw a television program about Asperger's syndrome, a disorder characterized by, among other things, the inability to read human emotions and a compensatory passion for objects and rituals. One of the little boys profiled on the program was obsessed with washers and dryers, another with trains, a third with game shows.

I do not have Asperger's syndrome. Even so, as I watched these boys—especially the one who spent so much of his time building cardboard miniatures of Speed Queen dryers—I found myself thrown back to the early days of my own childhood, when I developed a fascination with telephones. This began about the time that my parents replaced the rotary phones in our house with new push-button models. After that, I would find myself taking careful note, whenever I visited a new friend, of just how many phones his parents owned, what color they were, which style. Soon I had established a private ideal of how phones ought to be arranged, any digression from which—a Princess phone, say, in a kitchen—caused me real distress. Kitchens, according to my thinking, were supposed to have wall-mounted Slimlines. Princess phones belonged in bedrooms.

Another Asperger-like obsession from those days was with *Playboy* magazine, which I obliged my mother to buy me each month, less to satisfy some nascent erotic curiosity than because I so appreciated the reliability of the magazine's monthly features: the hidden bunny on the cover, the Vargas girl, the centerfold. In December I would lay out all twelve of that year's centerfolds on the family-room floor, then calculate how many of the playmates had been photographed from head to knee, how many from head to toe. This point of inconsistency—the fact that not every centerfold was photographed the same way—bothered me, especially when the two types of centerfolds could not be divided into six and six; for I had imposed upon the magazine the mandate never to stray from its precise geometry and therefore grew anxious at even the most minor detour.

It went on like that. Telephones and *Playboy* soon gave way to board games, soap operas, subways. When I was nine, on a visit to London, I rode the Underground all the way to Stanmore, not because there was anything to do in Stanmore but because it was the terminus of the Bakerloo (now the Jubilee) line, and I wanted to see what the end of the line looked like. (Later, this enthusiasm for the Underground led to a novel, *While England Sleeps*.)

Subway maps, which I collected in all the cities we visited and studied in earnest (memorizing the names of the stations, the number of interchanges, the points at which the trains came aboveground), provided a source of comfort during my adolescence, an escape route when stress or shyness overwhelmed me. Even as late as college, at moments of bewilderment I would resort to the old ritual of drawing imaginary subway systems, delineating with colored pens the different lines and taking care that in my world (as opposed to the real one) no two stations ever had the same name. Yet in retrospect I see that by making the transition from merely looking at maps to inventing them, I had crossed a crucial threshold. "Men make use of their illnesses," Aldous Huxley once wrote, "at least as much as they are made use of by them."

It was record albums that really showed me the way out. At first, when I started collecting them, I took less interest in their contents than in the principle according to which the songs on each one were arranged. Again, I imposed an arbitrary set of rules. I didn't like it if there were more songs on one side than the other; the songs had to be at least three minutes long, with a title that appeared in neither the first nor the last line. (If the title appeared in both the first and the last lines, I would remove the offending album from my shelf.) Then one afternoon my mother brought home from the library Grace Paley's *Enormous Changes at the Last Minute*. I took immediate notice. This was the first short-story collection I had ever seen, and skimming through it, what struck me instantly was its similarity to a record album. Here, too, short works were being gathered under a single title that at once accentuated their individuality and implied a common ground. And like the list of songs on the back of a record, the table of contents provided the book with its backbone: in Paley's case, the first three titles—"Wants," "Debts," "Distance"—sounded like a poem. Although it would be a while before I actually read Paley's stories, and even longer before their off-kilter poetry and generous

143

humor ignited in me the will to write my own, nonetheless the discovery of a new system to interrogate led me the next day to the library, where I found more story collections. And of course, within a matter of weeks, I wasn't only studying the tables of contents. I was reading them.

What got me excited, I see now, was the recognition that the imagination could impose upon ordinary life the very coherence that ordinary life so often fails to sustain. After all, no one could claim that the characters in Paley's stories led tidy lives. Yet the stories, the very shaping of the paragraphs, had an ordering effect on them; though the world might be messy, the sentences were lean, cohesive, beautiful. So I gave up seeking an elusive perfection in record albums and telephones, and started inventing.

This doesn't mean, of course, that even at thirty-nine there aren't days when I long to retreat from my work and look at telephone catalogs instead. That creativity lies just on the other side of madness is a commonplace, though popularly the madness with which art is associated is of the delusional variety, marked by visions and demons. Yet what of that more common writer's madness that calls to mind a windup robot that hits the wall and keeps walking? In *Middlemarch*, George Eliot limned the futility of vast totalizing projects, and in Mr. Casaubon, with his emotional illiteracy and blinkered devotion to an impossible "Key to All Mythologies," she created one of literature's first cases of Asperger's syndrome. Of course, all that distinguishes Eliot, who wrote many novels, from Mr. Casaubon, who never finished his "Key," is the saving grace of the imagination.

The Humble Genre
Novel, Sometimes Full
of Genius

∼

David Mamet

For the past thirty years the greatest novelists writing in English have been genre writers: John Le Carré, George Higgins and Patrick O'Brian.

Each year, of course, found the press discovering some writer whose style, provenance and choice of theme it found endearing. These usually trig, slim tomes shared a wistful and self-commendatory confusion at the multiplicity of life and stank of Art. But the genre writers wrote without sentimentality; their prose was concise and perceptive; in it the reader sees the life of which they wrote, rather than the writer's "technique."

For to hell with this putrid and despicable Graduate Degree sensitivity. Le Carré had been a spy, Higgins was a working lawyer and district attorney, and God knows what Patrick O'Brian had not been up to in his eighty-plus years.

Recently I put down O'Brian's sea novel *The Ionian Mission* and said to my wife, "This fellow has created characters and stories that are part of my life."

She said: "Write him a letter. He's in his eighties. Write him and thank him. And when you go to England, look him up, go tell him.

"How wonderful," she said, "to be alive, when he is still alive. Imagine living in the 1890s and being able to converse with Conan Doyle."

Well, I saw myself talking with Patrick O'Brian. "Sir," I would have said, "what a blow, the death of Barret Bonden." (Bonden, the coxswain, half-carries the wounded Captain Aubrey from the deck of a sinking privateer: "We'd best get back to the barky, sir, as this ship's going to Kingdom Come," the closing sentence of the novel.)

"Sir," I would have said, "I've read your Aubrey-Maturin series three or four times. When I was young I scoffed at stories of the Victorians who lived for the next issue of the *Strand* and the next tale of Sherlock Holmes; and I scoffed at the grown women and men who plagued Conan Doyle to rescind Holmes's death at the Reichenbach Falls. But I am blessed in having, in my generation, an equally thrilling set of heroes, and your characters have become a part of my life.

"Your minor characters," I would have said, "are especially dear to me: the mad Awkward Davis; Mrs. Fielding, the inexpert spy; old Mr. Herapath, the cowardly Boston loyalist; Christy-Palliere, the gallant French sea captain; and, of course, Barret Bonden, Captain Aubrey's coxswain." And I will not say I cried at his death, but I will not say I did not.

"And, Sir," I might have said, "I hope I do not overreach myself, but your prose is clear and spare as anyone could wish, quite as ironical as Mark Twain. . . ." And I hoped I should have the reserve to refrain from burdening him with a fan's fulsome, needless interpretation: that I could repay my debt with a straightforward statement of thanks.

The perfect medium for such, of course, is not the meeting, but the concise note.

So I sat at the breakfast table composing my note, and leafed through the newspaper and read of Patrick O'Brian's death.

His Aubrey-Maturin series, twenty novels of the Royal Navy in the Napoleonic Wars, is a masterpiece. It will outlive most of today's putative literary gems as Sherlock Holmes has outlived Bulwer-Lytton, as Mark Twain has outlived Charles Reade. God bless the straightforward writer, and God bless those with the ability to amuse, provoke, surprise, shock, appall.

The purpose of literature is to Delight. To create or endorse the Scholastic is a craven desire. It may yield a low-level self-satisfaction, but how can this compare with our joy at great, generous writing? With our joy of discovery of worth in the simple and straightforward? Is this Jingoism? The use of the term's a wish to side with the powerful, the Curator, the Editor. The schoolmaster's bad enough in the schoolroom; I prefer to keep him out of my bookshelf.

Henry Esmond was a genre piece, as were the Waverly novels, *Shadows on the Rock* and, if you will, both *Don Quixote* and *War and Peace*.

Ivan Albright's *That Which I Should Have Done I Did Not Do* is a genre painting: the decayed, grotesque door, hung with a funeral wreath. As a child I used to gaze at it, in the Art Institute in Chicago. "Yes," I would say to myself, "aha, yes, I understand."

I didn't, but I understand now.

Shel Silverstein said that there were some authors whose

books one wanted literally to hug to oneself: with thanks, and in unavailing protest that, at some point, the works had an end.

Trollope wrote that his imaginary Barsetshire was as real to him as any place in England, and that he was loath to leave it, but that that story was now done.

Patrick O'Brian, rest in peace.

She Was Blond. She Was in Trouble. And She Paid 3 Cents a Word

~

Ed McBain

There used to be a time when a person could make a decent living writing crime stories. Back then, a hardworking individual could earn 2 cents a word for a short story. Three cents, if he was exceptionally good. It beat polishing spittoons. Besides, it was fun.

Back then, starting a crime story was like reaching into a box of chocolates and being surprised by either the soft center or the caramel or the nuts. There were plenty of nuts in crime fiction, but you never knew what kind of story would come out of the machine until it started taking shape on the page. Like a jazz piano player, a good writer of short crime fiction didn't think he knew his job unless he could improvise in all twelve keys. Ringing variations on the theme was what made it such fun. Getting paid 2 or 3 cents a word was also fun.

For me, Private Eye stories were the easiest of the lot. All you had to do was talk out of the side of your mouth and get in trouble with the cops. In the PI stories back then, the cops were always heavies. If it weren't for the cops, the PI could solve a murder—any murder—in ten seconds flat. The cops were always dragging the PI into the cop shop to accuse him of having murdered somebody just because he happened to be at the scene of the crime before anybody else got there, sheesh!

I always started a PI story with a blonde wearing a tight shiny dress. When she crossed her legs, you saw rib-topped silk stockings and garters taut against milky white flesh, boy. Usually, she wanted to find her missing husband or somebody. Usually, the PI fell in love with her by the end of the story, but he had to be careful because you couldn't trust girls who crossed their legs to show their garters. A Private Eye was Superman wearing a fedora.

The Amateur Detective was a Private Eye without a license. The people who came to the Am Eye were usually friends or relatives who never dreamed of going to the police with a criminal problem but who couldn't afford to pay a private detective for professional help. So, naturally, they went to an amateur. They called upon a rabbi or a priest or the lady who was president of the garden club, or somebody who owned cats, or a guy who drove a locomotive on the Delaware Lackawanna, and they explained that somebody was missing, or dead, and could these busy amateurs please lend a helping hand?

Naturally, the garage mechanic, or the magician, or the elevator operator dropped everything to go help his friend or his maiden aunt. The Am Eye was smarter than either the PI or the cops because solving crimes wasn't his usual line of work, you see, but boy, was he good at it! It was fun writing Am Eye stories because you didn't have to know anything about criminal investigation. You just had to know all the station stops on the Delaware Lackawanna.

Even more fun was writing an Innocent Bystander story. You didn't have to know anything at all to write one of those. An Innocent Bystander story could be about anyone who witnessed a crime he or she should not have witnessed. Usually, this was a murder, but it could also be a kidnapping or an armed robbery or even spitting on the sidewalk, which is not a high crime, but which is probably a misdemeanor, go look it up. When you were writing an Innocent Bystander story, you didn't have to go look anything up. You witnessed a crime and went from there.

My good friend Otto Penzler, mystery connoisseur par excellence, insists that if any book, movie, play or poem has any sort of crime central to the plot, it is perforce a crime story. This would make *Hamlet* a crime story. *Macbeth*, too. In fact, this would make William Shakespeare the greatest crime writer of all time. But if his supposition is true, then spitting on the sidewalk would be a crime worthy of witness by an Innocent Bystander.

OK, the Innocent Bystander witnesses a heavyset gentleman clearing his throat and spitting on the sidewalk. He mutters something like, "Disgusting!" at which point a dozen men in black overcoats, all of them speaking in Middle European tongues, start chasing him, trying to murder or maim him or worse. At some point in the story, depending on how short it will be, the police could enter as well, accusing the Innocent Bystander of having been the one who'd spit on the sidewalk in the first place. It all turns out all right when a blonde wearing a shiny dress and flaunting rib-topped gartered silk stockings clears her throat and fluently explains everything in eight different foreign languages, thereby clearing up all the confusion as wedding bells chime.

It is better to be an Innocent Bystander than a Man on the Run or a Woman in Jeopardy, even though these three types of crime fiction are kissing cousins. The similarity they share is that the lead character in each of them is usually an innocent boob. The Innocent Bystander is, of course, innocent. Otherwise he would be a Guilty Bystander. But the Woman in Jeopardy is usually innocent as well. Her problem is that somebody is trying to do dire harm to her, we don't know why. Or if we do know why we also know this is all a terrible mistake, because she's innocent, can't you see she's innocent? If only we could tell this to the homicidal maniac who is chasing her day and night, trying to hurt her so badly.

Well, OK, in some of the stories she wasn't all that innocent. In some of the stories, she once did something sinful but not too terribly awful, which she was sorry for now but which this lunatic had blown up out of all proportion and was turning into a Federal case, shooting at her and trying to strangle her and everything. It was best, however, to make her a truly innocent little thing who didn't know why this deranged person was trying so hard to kill her. It was also good to give her any color hair but blond. There were no innocent blondes in crime fiction.

A Man on the Run was innocent, too, but the police (those guys again) didn't think so. In fact, they thought he'd done something very bad, and so they were chasing him. What they wanted to do was put him in the electric chair or send him away for life. And, so, naturally, he was running.

The thing we didn't know was whether or not he really was guilty. We certainly hoped he wasn't because he seemed like a personable enough fellow, although a bit sweaty from running all the time.

But maybe he was guilty, who knew? Maybe the cops—those rotten individuals—were right for a change. All we knew for sure was that this man was running. Very fast. So fast that we hardly had time to wonder was he guilty, was he innocent, was he in the marathon? The only important thing a writer had to remember was that before the man could stop running, he had to catch the guy who really did what the reader was hoping he didn't do, but which the police were sure he did do. At 3 cents a word, the longer he ran, the better off the writer was.

Cops.

When I first started writing the Cop Story, I knew only one thing about policemen: they were inhuman beasts. The problem was how to turn them into likable, sympathetic human beings. The answer was simple. Give them head colds. And first names. And keep their dialogue homey and conversational. Natural-sounding people with runny noses and first names had to be at least as human as you and I were. Keeping all this firmly in mind, writing a sympathetic Cop Story became a simple matter.

"Good morning, Mrs. Flaherty, is this here your husband's body with the ice pick sticking out of his ear here?"

"Yes, that is my dearest George."

"Excuse me, ma'am, I have to blow my nose."

"Go right ahead, detective."

"When did you catch that cold, Harry?"

"I've had it for a week now, Dave."

"Lots of it going around."

"My husband, George, here had a bad cold, too, was why he stuck the ice pick in his own ear."

"What have you been taking for it, Harry?"

"The wife made me some chicken soup, Dave."

"Yeah, chicken soup's always good for a cold."

"Oh dear, just look at all that blood."

"Sure is a sight, ma'am."

"Didn't know a person could bleed that much from the ear, did you?"

"No, ma'am, I surely did not."

"Mind your foot, ma'am. You're stepping in it."

"Oh dear."

"Hot milk and butter's supposed to be good, too."

"Medical Examiner should be here any minute, Harry. Maybe he can give you something for it."

"I miss him so much."

Once you humanized cops, everyone could understand exactly how good of heart and decent they were, and the rest was easy.

The hardest story to write was what was called Biter Bit. As the name suggests, this is a story in which the perpetrator unwittingly becomes the victim. For example, I make an elaborate plan to shoot you, but when I open the door to your bedroom, you're standing there with a pistol in your hand, and you shoot me. Biter Bit.

I once had a wonderful idea for a Biter Bit story. This writer keeps submitting stories to the same editor who hates his work and who keeps rejecting them with a little slip saying, "Needs work." So the writer writes a story titled "Needs Work," and he puts it in a manila envelope rigged with a letter bomb, which he mails to the despised editor, hoping to read in the next day's newspaper that the man has been blown to smithereens. Instead, there's a letter from the editor in the writer's mailbox, and when he opens the envelope, it explodes.

I know.

It needs work.

Virtual Reality: The Perils of Seeking a Novelist's Facts in Her Fiction

Sue Miller

Before my last, recent book tour, I made myself memorize a quotation from an interview with John Cheever that began, "It seems to me that any confusion between autobiography and fiction debases fiction." Thus girded, armored, I hoped to silence forever the questioner who sits there in the third row waiting to ask, "How much of your work is autobiographical?"

I'd go on, quoting away: "The role autobiography plays in fiction is like that of reality to a dream. As you dream your ship, you perhaps know the boat, but you're going towards a coast that is quite strange; you're wearing strange clothes, the language being spoken around you is a language you don't understand, but the woman on the left is your wife."

Take that!

Only it didn't work. What I got back, in one form or another, was: "OK, sure. But really, how much?" What's more, a friend who came to one of the readings told me that I'd been unkind, that I'd seemed contemptuous of someone who was, after all, simply and genuinely curious. Which made me wonder: Why did it bother me so much, that recurring question? Far more than the question about my work habits or the one about whether I use a computer or not.

Here's what I think: It bothers me because I sense in it a kind of potential diminishment—yes, debasing—of the work I do. What the questioner seems to be somehow suggesting is that my writing is possibly no more than the stringing together of episodes lifted directly from my life, or from the lives of fascinating characters I have known.

Every writer has met the guy at the party who says he, too, has always wanted to write a novel, if only he had the time, because he's got such a great story to tell. And it seems to me that it's that same guy asking the question at the reading. Maybe this is why the question arises so often: because the guy really wants to know how to do it, how to make fiction from the interesting or painful or shocking things that have happened to him.

There's a way in which readers are encouraged in this by writers who embrace the cult of experience, the notion that the writer needs to have lived a certain kind of bold, engaged life, right out there on the edge of . . . well, something or other, in order to have anything worthwhile to write about. What's worthwhile? Well, war, for instance. Adventure on the high seas, or the highways, or the river. The gutter life in Paris, the drug life in New York. No wonder anyone who has even marginally partaken of any of these feels justified in thinking he must have a book in him. Somewhere.

But if experience were all, we would all have a book. As Flannery O'Connor said, anyone who's survived infancy has enough material for countless stories. The fact is, you can make a story of anything, anything at all. What's hard—and what's interesting—about a story is not so much the thing that's in it, but what's made of that thing. And then, of course, the making itself. But there is no necessary life to have lived or scene to have witnessed. No experiential sine qua non. As Henry James said of the material of fiction, "Why . . . adventure, more than . . . matrimony, or celibacy, or parturition, or cholera?"

Women, more than men, seem always to have known this, perhaps because they have until relatively recently written out of constrained lives, limited worlds: for the most part, in fact, the worlds of matrimony and celibacy and parturition. They had to learn to notice everything, to make much from little. Too little, it has seemed to some critics. No writer of the domestic, female or male, could please the likes of Tom Wolfe, for instance. When I read his prescriptions for contemporary fiction, I remember Cheever bemoaning the size of his own gift in comparison with Bellow's, regretting his homely material, wishing for the sweep of *Augie March* or *Henderson*.

So is the life's shape the shape of the fiction then? Is it all autobiographical? Is that what Cheever was suffering from? Do I write as I do because I've lived and worked primarily with children and families? Is it true that we have no choice but to echo what's happened to us and to those we know? Do we writers need to shed our bathrobes, get dressed at last and shuffle blinking out of our studies into the bright light of day, find jobs as laborers or insurance executives or physicians or models or pimps in order to have something wilder, something more exciting, something more relevant to contemporary life to write about?

Surely not. Surely the writer's job is to make relevant the world she wishes to write about. How? By writing well and carefully and powerfully. By using humor, as Cheever did; or violence, as O'Connor did; or rue, as Chekhov did, to make the territory of her imagination compelling and somehow universal. And that holds true whether the territory of the imagination is close to the literal truth of her life or far from it.

Sometimes the distance is minimal, minimal enough for the fiction to cause lifelong hard feelings: the use of a fictional alter ego, for example, or of changes so slight that they seem like a kind of cruel joke. Sometimes, especially with what is called domestic fiction—fiction practiced in one way or another by Updike, Munro, Roth, Carver, Ford, McDermott—family or friends can end up feeling misused, abused. There are certainly writers who seem nearly deliberately provocative in this way: the burning-bridges school of art.

For the true writer, though, however close the events may be to his life, there is some distance, some remove, that allows for the shaping of the work. The shaping, after all, is what it's all about. Every reader can sense the difference between a writer who embodies meaning through the events he describes and the writer who seems simply mired in those events. It is that struggle for meaning that lets the writer escape the tyranny of what really happened and begin to dream his fictional dream.

As to what happens in the dream, in the story, well, we all have the kinds of event we prefer, but surely this is a matter of preference, not worth. You find in the story of a quest for a white whale the embodiment of the human struggle for control, for wholeness? Fine. For me everyday life in the hands of a fine writer seems similarly charged with meaning. When I write, I want to bring a sense of that charge, that meaning, to what may fairly be called the domestic. OK?

So, come on, really, how much is autobiographical?

All of it. None.

For Authors, Fragile Ideas Need Loving Every Day

Walter Mosley

If you want to be a writer, you have to write every day. The consistency, the monotony, the certainty, all vagaries and passions are covered by this daily reoccurrence.

You don't go to a well once but daily. You don't skip a child's breakfast or forget to wake up in the morning. Sleep comes to you each day, and so does the muse.

She comes softly and quietly, behind your left ear or in a corner of the next room. Her words are whispers, her ideas shifting renditions of possibilities that have not been resolved, though they have occurred and reoccurred a thousand times in your mind. She, or it, is a collection of memories not exactly your own.

These reminiscences surface in dreams or out of abstract notions brought on by tastes and excitations, failures and hopes that you experience continually. These ideas have no physical form. They are smoky concepts liable to disappear at the slightest disturbance. An alarm clock or a ringing telephone will dispel a new character; answering the call will erase a chapter from the world.

Our most precious ability, the knack of creation, is also our most fleeting resource. What might be fades in the world of necessity.

How can I create when I have to go to work, cook my dinner, remember what I did wrong to the people who have stopped calling? And even if I do find a moment here and there—a weekend away in the mountains, say—how can I say everything I need to say before the world comes crashing back with all of its sirens and shouts and television shows?

"I know I have a novel in me," I often hear people say. "But how can I get it out?"

The answer is, always is, every day.

The dream of the writer, of any artist, is a fickle and amorphous thing. One evening you're remembering a homeless man, dressed in clothes that smelled like cheese rinds, who you once stood next to on a street corner in New York. Your memory becomes a reverie, and in this daydream you ask him where he's from. With a thick accent he tells you that he was born in Hungary, that he was a freedom fighter, but that now, here in America, his freedom has deteriorated into the poverty of the streets.

You write down a few sentences in your journal and sigh. This exhalation is not exhaustion but anticipation at the prospect of a wonderful tale exposing a notion that you still only partly understand.

A day goes by. Another passes. At the end of the next week you find yourself in the same chair, at the same hour when you wrote about the homeless man previously. You open the journal to see what you'd written. You remember everything perfectly, but the life has somehow drained out of it. The words have no art to them; you no longer remember the smell. The idea seems weak, it has dissipated, like smoke.

This is the first important lesson that the writer must learn. Writing a novel is gathering smoke. It's an excursion into the ether of ideas. There's no time to waste. You must work with that idea as well as you can, jotting down notes and dialogue.

The first day the dream you gathered will linger, but it won't last long. The next day you have to return to tend to your flimsy vapors. You have to brush them, reshape them, breathe into them and gather more.

It doesn't matter what time of day you work, but you have to work every day because creation, like life, is always slipping away from you. You must write every day, but there's no time limit on how long you have to write.

One day you might read over what you've done and think about it. You pick up the pencil or turn on the computer, but no new words come. That's fine. Sometimes you can't go further. Correct a misspelling, reread a perplexing paragraph, and then let it go. You have reentered the dream of the work, and that's enough to keep the story alive for another twenty-four hours.

The next day you might write for hours; there's no way to tell. The goal is not a number of words or hours spent writing. All you need is to keep your heart and mind open to the work.

Nothing we create is art at first. It's simply a collection of notions that may never be understood. Returning every day

163

thickens the atmosphere. Images appear. Connections are made. But even these clearer notions will fade if you stay away more than a day.

Reality fights against your dreams, it tries to deny creation and change. The world wants you to be someone known, someone with solid ideas, not blowing smoke. Given a day, reality will begin to scatter your notions; given two days, it will drive them off.

The act of writing is a kind of guerrilla warfare; there is no vacation, no leave, no relief. In actuality there is very little chance of victory. You are, you fear, like that homeless man, likely to be defeated by your fondest dreams.

But then the next day comes, and the words are waiting. You pick up where you left off, in the cool and shifting mists of morning.

To Invigorate Literary Mind, Start Moving Literary Feet

~

Joyce Carol Oates

Running! If there's any activity happier, more exhilarating, more nourishing to the imagination, I can't think what it might be. In running the mind flies with the body; the mysterious efflorescence of language seems to pulse in the brain, in rhythm with our feet and the swinging of our arms. Ideally, the runner who's a writer is running through the land- and cityscapes of her fiction, like a ghost in a real setting.

There must be some analogue between running and dreaming. The dreaming mind is usually bodiless, has peculiar powers of locomotion and, in my experience at least, often runs or glides or "flies" along the ground or in the air. (Leaving aside the blunt, deflating theory that dreams are merely compensatory: you fly in sleep because in life you crawl, barely; you're soaring above others in sleep because in life others soar above you.)

Possibly these fairy-tale feats of locomotion are atavistic remnants, the hallucinatory memory of a distant ancestor for whom the physical being, charged with adrenaline in emergency situations, was indistinguishable from the spiritual or intellectual. In running, "spirit" seems to pervade the body; as musicians experience the uncanny phenomenon of tissue memory in their fingertips, so the runner seems to experience in feet, lungs, quickened heartbeat, an extension of the imagining self.

The structural problems I set for myself in writing, in a long, snarled, frustrating and sometimes despairing morning of work, for instance, I can usually unsnarl by running in the afternoon.

On days when I can't run, I don't feel "myself"; and whoever the "self" is I feel, I don't like nearly so much as the other. And the writing remains snarled in endless revisions.

Writers and poets are famous for loving to be in motion. If not running, hiking; if not hiking, walking. (Walking, even fast, is a poor second to running, as all runners know, what we'll resort to when our knees go. But at least it's an option.)

The English romantic poets were clearly inspired by their long walks, in all weather: Wordsworth and Coleridge in the idyllic Lake District, for instance; Shelley ("I always go until I am stopped and I never am stopped") in his four intense years in Italy. The New England transcendentalists, most famously Henry David Thoreau, were ceaseless walkers; Thoreau boasted of having "traveled much in Concord," and in his eloquent essay "Walking" acknowledged that he had to spend more than four hours out of doors daily, in motion; otherwise he felt "as if I had some sin to be atoned for."

My favorite prose on the subject is Charles Dickens's "Night Walks," which he wrote some years after having suffered extreme insomnia that propelled him out into the

London streets at night. Written with Dickens's usual brilliance, this haunting essay seems to hint at more than its words reveal. He associates his terrible night restlessness with what he calls "houselessness": under a compulsion to walk and walk and walk in the darkness and pattering rain. (No one has captured the romance of desolation, the ecstasy of near-madness, more forcibly than Dickens, so wrongly interpreted as a dispenser of popular, softhearted tales.)

It isn't surprising that Walt Whitman should have tramped impressive distances, for you can feel the pulse beat of the walker in his slightly breathless, incantatory poems. But it may be surprising to learn that Henry James, whose prose style more resembles the fussy intricacies of crocheting than the fluidity of movement, also loved to walk for miles in London.

I, too, walked (and ran) for miles in London years ago. Much of it in Hyde Park. Regardless of weather. Living for a sabbatical year with my husband, an English professor, in a corner of Mayfair overlooking Speaker's Corner, I was so afflicted with homesickness for America, and for Detroit, I ran compulsively; not as a respite for the intensity of writing but as a function of writing.

As I ran, I was running in Detroit, envisioning the city's parks and streets, avenues and expressways, with such eidetic clarity I had only to transcribe them when I returned to our flat, re-creating Detroit in my novel *Do With Me What You Will* as faithfully as I'd re-created Detroit in *Them* when I was living there.

What a curious experience! Without the bouts of running, I don't believe I could have written the novel; yet how perverse, one thinks, to be living in one of the world's most beautiful cities, London, and to be dreaming of one of the world's most problematic cities, Detroit. But of course, as no one has yet remarked in this diverse and idiosyncratic series, *Writers on Writing*, writers are crazy.

Each of us, we like to think, in her own inimitable way.

Both running and writing are highly addictive activities; both are, for me, inextricably bound up with consciousness. I can't recall a time when I wasn't running, and I can't recall a time when I wasn't writing.

(Before I could write what might be called human words in the English language, I eagerly emulated grown-ups' handwriting in pencil scribbles. My first "novels"—which I'm afraid my loving parents still have, in a trunk or a drawer on our old farm property in Millersport, New York— were tablets of inspired scribbles illustrated by line drawings of chickens, horses and upright cats. For I had not yet mastered the trickier human form, as I was years from mastering human psychology.)

My earliest outdoor memories have to do with the special solitude of running or hiking in our pear and apple orchards, through fields of wind-rustling corn towering over my head, along farmers' lanes and on bluffs above the Tonawanda Creek. Through childhood I hiked, roamed, tirelessly explored the countryside: neighboring farms, a treasure trove of old barns, abandoned houses and forbidden properties of all kinds, some of them presumably dangerous, like cisterns and wells covered with loose boards.

These activities are intimately bound up with storytelling, for always there's a ghost-self, a "fictitious" self, in such settings. For this reason I believe that any form of art is a species of exploration and transgression. (I never saw a "No Trespassing" sign that wasn't a summons to my rebellious blood. Such signs, dutifully posted on trees and fence railings, might as well cry, "Come Right In!")

To write is to invade another's space, if only to memorialize it. To write is to invite angry censure from those who don't write, or who don't write in quite the way you do, for whom you may seem a threat. Art by its nature is a transgressive act, and artists must accept being punished for it. The more original and unsettling their art, the more devastating the punishment.

If writing involves punishment, at least for some of us, the act of running even in adulthood can evoke painful memories of having been, long ago, as children, chased by tormentors. (Is there any adult who hasn't such memories? Are there any adult women who have not been, in one way or another, sexually molested or threatened?) That adrenaline rush, like an injection to the heart!

I attended a one-room country schoolhouse in which eight very disparate grades were taught by a single overworked woman. The teasing, pummeling, pinching, punching, mauling, kicking and verbal abuse that surrounded the relative sanctuary of the schoolhouse simply had to be endured, for in those days there were no protective laws against such mistreatment. This was a laissez-faire era in which a man might beat the daylights out of his wife and children, and the police would rarely intervene except in cases of serious injury or death.

Often when I'm running in the most idyllic landscapes, I'm reminded of the panicked childhood running of decades ago. I was one of those luckless children without older brothers or sisters to protect her against the systematic cruelty of older classmates, thus fair game. I don't believe I was singled out (because my grades were high, for instance), and I came to see years later that such abuse is generic, not personal. It must prevail through the species; it allows us insight into the experiences of others, a sense of what a more enduring panic, entrapment, suffering and despair must be truly like. Sexual abuse seems to us the most repellent kind of abuse, and it's certainly the abuse that nourishes a palliative amnesia.

Beyond the lines of printed words in my books are the settings in which the books were imagined and without which the books could not exist. Sometime in 1985, for instance, running along the Delaware River south of Yardley, Pennsylvania, I glanced up and saw the ruins of a railroad bridge and experienced in a flash such a vivid, visceral memory of crossing a footbridge beside a similar railroad trestle high above the Erie Canal in Lockport, New York, when I was twelve to fourteen years old, that I saw the possibility of a novel. This would become *You Must Remember This*, set in a mythical upstate New York city very like the original.

Yet often the reverse occurs: I find myself running in a place so intriguing to me, amid houses, or the backs of houses, so mysterious, I'm fated to write about these sights, to bring them to life (as it's said) in fiction. I'm a writer absolutely mesmerized by places; much of my writing is a way of assuaging homesickness, and the settings my characters inhabit are as crucial to me as the characters themselves. I couldn't write even a very short story without vividly "seeing" what its characters see.

Stories come to us as wraiths requiring precise embodiments. Running seems to allow me, ideally, an expanded consciousness in which I can envision what I'm writing as a film or a dream. I rarely invent at the typewriter but recall what I've experienced. I don't use a word processor but write in longhand, at considerable length. (Again, I know: writers are crazy.)

By the time I come to type out my writing formally, I've envisioned it repeatedly. I've never thought of writing as the mere arrangement of words on the page but as the attempted embodiment of a vision: a complex of emotions, raw experience.

The effort of memorable art is to evoke in the reader or spectator emotions appropriate to that effort. Running is a meditation; more practicably it allows me to scroll through, in my mind's eye, the pages I've just written, proofreading for errors and improvements.

My method is one of continuous revision. While writing a long novel, every day I loop back to earlier sections to rewrite, in order to maintain a consistent, fluid voice. When I write the final two or three chapters of a novel, I write them simultaneously with the rewriting of the opening, so that, ideally at least, the novel is like a river uniformly flowing, each passage concurrent with all the others.

My most recent novel is twelve hundred finished manuscript pages, which means many more typed-out pages, and how many miles of running, I dare not guess!

Dreams may be temporary flights into madness that, by some law of neurophysiology unclear to us, keep us from actual madness. So, too, the twin activities of running and writing keep the writer reasonably sane and with the hope, however illusory and temporary, of control.

A Storyteller Stands Where Justice Confronts Basic Human Needs

~

Sara Paretsky

Some months ago I had a letter from a reader who was so furious she covered four pages by hand, demanding to know why my books were "infested" with political issues. "When I buy a mystery, I expect to be entertained," she wrote, "and when you bring in all that stuff about homeless people, you aren't entertaining me."

I thought of writing back to say that mysteries are political. Peter Wimsey staunchly defends an England where everyone knows his (or her) place and is happy in it. Philip Marlowe and Sam Spade inhabit a landscape filled with explicit sexual politics. Raymond Chandler's women reek of sex, as Marlowe complains in *The Little Sister*; Dashiell Hammett's women, like Brigid O'Shaughnessy, try to make good boys do bad things. But Marlowe and Spade are both too moral for them.

Mysteries, like cops, are right up against the place where people's basest and basic needs intersect with law and justice. They are by definition political. That's one reason I like to write them as well as read them.

In the end, though, it seemed too hard to explain this in a letter, so I did what I usually do with such an angry reader: sent the woman the price of a book and got on with my work, which is as a storyteller, a writer whose stories take place in the world of law, justice and society.

I thought of my correspondent again later, when I was giving a reading at the Newberry Library in Chicago. A group of nine women stayed until everyone else had left. They told me then that they were married to steelworkers, to men who had not been able to find work for more than a decade as the global economy sent their jobs out of the country. They themselves were working two jobs to keep roofs over their families and food on the tables. These weren't great jobs; a neighborhood with 50 percent unemployment doesn't run to great jobs. They were cashiers at convenience stores or waitresses in diners. They told me they hadn't read a book since they graduated from high school, until one of them heard on the radio that the heroine of my detective novels, V. I. Warshawski, came from their own neighborhood, South Chicago. V. I. grew up under the shadow of the steel mills. She went to the University of Chicago on scholarship, but she's a blue-collar gal. The women at my reading said they had never thought that a book could tell them something about their lives until they read one of mine. "We buy them in hardcover," one of them said. "V. I. helps us face the terrible things that have happened to our lives."

My first impulse was to say, no, don't put your hard-earned money into a hardcover book. But fortunately I had the grace not to blurt that out, to see that buying the books was an important physical touchstone.

My next, meaner-spirited impulse, was to go back to the woman who'd written me and say, see, this is the point: I'm a storyteller, I'm an entertainer, but the stories that come to me are almost always those of voiceless people, not those of the powerful. These South Chicago women were entertained, they had a few hours' escape from the relentless round of work, housecleaning, angry depressed husbands, adolescent sons who couldn't find jobs, daughters marrying too young with nothing to live on. My books entertained them, but they also gave them courage.

I don't like social-political novels, books written only to make a point to show that four legs are better than two, or all males are testosterone-crazed villains, or that women invariably use their bodies to subvert male morality. There's a reason that the writers we know from Stalin's Soviet Union are Pasternak and Akhmatova, not Gribachev, who wrote *Spring in the Victory Collective Farm*. Pasternak may have wanted to make a point, a most ardently felt point, about human freedom, about the confusion that one feels in the midst of social upheavals and how hard it is to know how to act. But he wanted to write about human beings caught up in events, not idealized political types.

I don't sit down to write books of social or political commentary. Both as a reader and a writer, I'm pulled by stories, not by ideas; I see the world in the stories of the people around me. It's just that the stories that speak most to me are those of people like the women from South Chicago who can't speak for themselves, who feel powerless and voiceless in the larger world. It may be that all writers come to their craft from a sense of being on the margins of life, of seeing the world with an outsider's eye and needing to make sense of it. Certainly that was true of those master story-tellers Dickens and Eliot, and I suppose it's true of me as well.

I grew up in the '50s, in eastern Kansas, in a time and place that contemporary moralists point at as the golden era in America, before Vietnam and drugs and feminism and black power caused permanent upheaval in our land-scape.

It was a time and place where we girls knew our inevitable destiny was marriage, where only bad girls had sex beforehand and then reaped our inevitable punishment. I grew up the only girl in a household of boys, where my parents—eccentric outsiders in a Protestant and Republican landscape when it came to religion or to civil rights—conformed rigidly in their sexual politics. Home was for me personally, specifically, a place where my value lay in house-work and baby-sitting, not in an education leading to the careers envisioned for boys. I grew up barely able to speak above a whisper, so fearful I was of the criticism that dogged almost anything I said or did. I retreated young into the world of stories, of happy endings, for the heroines I cre-ated, as well as the ones I read about.

When I first escaped from that milieu, it was to come to Chicago in the late '60s. The same summer that the Rev. Dr. Martin Luther King Jr. was trying to organize for open housing and equal pay in Chicago, I arrived to do commu-nity service work on the city's South Side. He was organiz-ing near the blue-collar, mostly Lithuanian and Polish neighborhood where I had been assigned.

I didn't then and don't now hold any brief for the fears that turned into bottle-throwing, car-burning hate in

Marquette Park that summer, or led whites to sell their five-room homes at a loss and flee in terror for the western suburbs. But even at nineteen I could see that neither the banks, the real estate agents, nor the city government cared one iota about the dreams or fears centered on those tiny bungalows. Everyone around me felt powerless, the blacks denied access to jobs and decent housing, the whites living just half a rung above on the economic ladder and clinging to it in panic.

That summer I felt a sort of desperate need to start writing down the lives of people without voices. Instead of princesses who lived happily ever after, after that summer I began writing about ordinary people whose lives, like mine, were filled with the anomie that comes from having no voice, no power. Even then I still felt so voiceless myself that it was another twelve years before I tried to sell my work: so fully had I absorbed the indoctrination of my Kansas childhood that I couldn't imagine myself writing outside the home, couldn't imagine that my words might speak to other people.

Dickens moved from the remotest margin—the debtor's prison—to the center of the Victorian page, as the most-sought-out man of his age. The big house, servants, important visitors, high-fee lecture tours, five-figure contracts never brought him security. Nor did they obscure for him the underpinnings of Victorian affluence: the array of homeless children without nutrition or education, sweatshops, crime arising out of pressures of the vilest poverty.

Dickens romanticized the virtues of the poor, but he didn't sentimentalize the circumstances of their poverty. His books are, as my letter writer put it, infested with social politics, but people still lined up by the thousands on the wharves in Boston to wait for the ship that was bringing the next installment of his work.

One hundred fifty years later we still live an affluent life with an array of homeless children suffering from malnutrition and maleducation under our noses: the elephant in the living room we all ignore. A century after my grandparents met walking a picket line for the ILGWU we still have sweatshops in this great land of ours. We still have crime, homelessness, parents selling their children for a nickel bag and a host of other ills. If a master storyteller like Dickens could find his most compelling stories within that landscape, who am I to turn away from it?

Life of Prose and Poetry: An Inspiring Combination

~

Marge Piercy

Whenever I face an audience with at least minimal familiarity with my work, there are two questions always asked: "Why do you write both fiction and poetry?" "What's the difference between writing poetry and fiction?"

I have various glib answers I whip out of my failing brain. I mention that while it may be rarer for men to cross genre lines, some, like Richard Price, who produces fiction and film scripts, do. However, many women work in more than one genre, and then I rattle off a list: Margaret Atwood, Erica Jong, Adrienne Rich, Alice Walker, Rita Dove, Colleen McElroy, Nikki Giovanni, Joan Didion, Lillian Hellman, Linda Hogan; and that's without trying hard.

Sometimes I say that if a writer works in more than one genre, the chances of getting writer's block are greatly diminished. If I am stuck in a difficult passage of a novel, I may jump ahead to smoother ground, or I may pause and work on poems exclusively for a time. If I lack ideas for one genre, usually I have them simmering for the other.

I am always going back and forth. It's a rare period that is devoted only to one. That happens when I am revising a novel to a deadline, working every day until my eyes or my back gives out, and when I am putting a collection of poetry together, making a coherent artifact out of the poems of the last few years and reworking them as I go.

I see this essay as an opportunity to ask myself about writing both poetry and fiction in a more incisive way. Poetry feels as if I transcend myself while working on what is often very personal material. When I am fully engaged in writing a poem, the "I" is less intrusive, less present than at any other time except deep meditation. But the intense concentration of making a poem is quite different from the intense focus of mediation, because rather than clearing the mind, the mind is wildly busy and open. The stray images and thoughts that the mediator blows away are the rich suggestive stuff of poems. Every little gnat of irrelevancy may turn out to be what the poem is really about.

Some poems come entire, bless them, dictated by the muse or *ha-Shem* or the tooth fairy. They arrive. They may be important or trivial. When I am discussing inspiration with students, some of whom always want to overvalue the spontaneous, I tell the old chestnut about the Boston Brahmin who woke in the middle of the night from the revelation of the truth of human relationships, wrote down the awesome words and in the morning found, "Higgamous piggamous, men are polygamous; hoggamous, poggamous, women, monogamous."

Poems start from a phrase, an image, an idea, a rhythm insistent in the back of the brain. I once wrote a poem when I realized I had been hearing a line from a David Byrne song entirely wrong, and I liked it my way. Some poems are a journey of discovery and exploration for the writer as well as the reader. I find out where I am going when I finally arrive, which may take years.

Poems hatch from memory, fantasy, the need to communicate with the living, the dead, the unborn. Poems come directly out of daily life, from the garden, the cats, the newspaper, the lives of friends, quarrels, a good or bad time in bed, from cooking, from writing itself, from disasters and nuisances, gifts and celebrations. They go back into daily life: people read them at weddings and funerals, give them to lovers or soon-to-be ex-lovers or those they lust for, put them up on their refrigerators or over their computers, use them to teach or to exhort, to vent joy or grief.

The mind wraps itself around a poem. It is almost sensual, particularly if you work on a computer. You can turn the poem round and about and upside down, dancing with it a kind of bolero of two snakes twisting and coiling, until the poem has found its right and proper shape.

There is something so personal and so impersonal at once in the activity that it is addictive. I may be dealing with my own anger, my humiliation, my passion, my pleasure; but once I am working with it in a poem, it becomes molten ore. It becomes "not me." And the being who works with it is not the normal, daily me. It has no sex, no shame, no ambition, no net. It eats silence like bread. I can't stay in that white-hot place long, but when I am in it, there is nothing else. All the dearness and detritus of ordinary living falls away, even when that is the stuff of the poem. It is as remote as if I were an archaeologist working with the kitchen midden of a four-thousand-year-old city.

Prose is prosier. No high-flying language here. My urge to write fiction comes from the same part of my psyche that cannot resist eavesdropping on strangers' conversations in airports, in restaurants, in the supermarket. I am a nosy person. My mother was an amazing listener, and she radiated something that caused strangers on buses to sit down and begin to tell her their life stories or their troubles. I have learned to control that part of myself, but I am still a good interviewer and a good listener because I am madly curious about what people's lives are like and what they think about them and say about them and the silences between the words.

I always want to hear how the stories come out, what happens next, a basic urge all writers bring to fiction and one pull that keeps readers turning page after page. Another drive is the desire to make sense of the random, chaotic, painful, terrifying, astonishing events of our lives. We want there to be grand patterns. We want there to be some sense in events, even if the sense is that no one is in charge and entropy conquers; that all is illusion or a baroque and tasteless joke. Each good novel has a vision of its world that informs what is put in and what is left out.

I write character-centered fiction, which means it is almost never high concept, and my plots are neither tight nor ingenious. I get to know my major characters very well indeed before I write a word of the novel. Most of what happens simply proceeds from the interaction of the characters with one another and their environment, their history, their circumstances.

Some of my training as a novelist came from listening to adults, mostly women, talk, eavesdropping on gossip and scandal. My mother read palms and dispensed advice freely but clandestinely, for my father would have been furious if he had known. He disliked irrationality. I overheard and pondered: What did Mrs. G. walk in on between her husband and her sister? Why did Mr. A. disappear after he hit on the numbers? Why did my mother sigh whenever she mentioned the young woman next door?

My other early training was in the importance of viewpoint. My grandmother Hannah, who lived with us part of every year and shared my bed in our tiny house, was a storyteller in the shtetl mold. She told me tales of the golem, Lilith, dybbuks, flying rabbis, but also stories of our extended family. My mother told those stories, too, but quite differently. If I heard the same story from my Aunt Ruth, who was midway in age between my mother and me and more like my girlfriend than my other aunts, there were three versions of every story: the spiritual and moralistic, the sensational and dramatic, and the factual, exactly what happened and what was the evidence for various opinions.

For me the gifts of the novelist are empathy and imagination. I enter my characters and try to put on their worldviews, their ways of moving, their habits, their beliefs and the lies they tell themselves, their passions and antipathies, even the language in which they speak and think: the colors of their lives. Imagination has to do with moving those characters through events, has to do with entering another time, whether of the recent past or three hundred or five hundred years ago, in Prague or Paris or London or New York or the islands of the Pacific. It has to do with changing some variables and moving into imagined futures, while retaining a sense of character so strong the reader will believe in a landscape and in cities and worlds vastly different from our own.

Do the genres ever overlap? Oddly enough, fiction and poetry approach most closely when I am doing research for a novel. I have a series of poems in *Available Light* that come from researching *Gone to Soldiers*, finding the precise places where certain events happened during World War II.

The sense of place is extremely important to me in being able to enter a character's past or present. I may not need long in a city or in a landscape, just a matter of hours or days; but without that immersion, the writing is much harder. Out of these journeys poems arise, sometimes directly, finding the exact spot through a maze of logging roads in the Montagne Noir where the Armée Juive met the Germans in battle, from surviving descriptions; sometimes accidentally, as in encountering a hungry dog outside the ramparts of Aigues-Mortes, giving him a baguette as a joke and being shamed by his joy and pride in his find.

Ideas for poems come to me any old time, but not generally ideas for revising poems. The notion that revising poems is a different process from revising fiction occurred to me on the treadmill, but I cannot imagine that I would ever think about actually revising a poem there. When I rewrite a poem, I go back into the space of the poem and contemplate it. I read it aloud. The only other time when I work on revising a poem is the first or second time I read it to an audience, when all the weak and incoherent parts suddenly manifest themselves big as the writing on billboards.

With fiction, since I live inside a novel for two or three years, the problem is letting go when I am done for the day. Ideas for what I am working on come in the night, in the tub, on planes, in the middle of supper. I keep a notebook on the night table, so that when an idea bombs in at 2 A.M., I will not get up and turn on the computer. One reason I learned to meditate was to control my fictional imagination and not let the characters take me over. Learning to let go except for those occasional flashes is central to keeping my sanity and my other, real relationships.

Lastly, I perform poetry regularly for audiences and thus enjoy the same feedback a musician does: applause, emotional response, that heat a crowd whose attention you have captured gives off. With fiction I am dependent on fan mail and critical articles. Although people have asked me to write a novel for them about their lives, I have never been tempted. But with poetry I have written poems for occasions, as most poets do. I have also written liturgy that is used by some Reconstructionist and Reform congregations and also Unitarian poetry intended for public performance by people who are not poets. I think poetry ultimately is a more communal activity than fiction, but I love both equally.

Inspiration? Head Down the Back Road, and Stop for the Yard Sales

~

Annie Proulx

The Irish singer Christy Moore clips out "Don't Forget Your Shovel," a song I like not only for its tripping rhythm and sly social commentary but for its advice to the diggers of the world, a group to which I belong.

A whole set of metaphoric shovels is part of my tool collection, and for me the research that underlies the writing is the best part of the scribbling game. Years ago, alder scratched, tired, hungry, and on a late return from a fishing trip, I was driving through Maine when a hubbub on the sidewalk caught my eye: milling customers at a yard sale. I stop for yard sales.

Pay dirt. I found the wonderful second edition unabridged *Webster's New International Dictionary* with its rich definitions and hundreds of fine small illustrations. On a collapsing card table nearby sat *Harper's Dictionary of Classical Literature and Antiquities*, *The Oxford Companion to English Literature*, and other weighty reference works, discards from a local library and the best catch of the trip.

I am an inveterate buyer of useful books on all possible subjects. Collectors pass up ex-libris books, but I need reading copies. And because I often fold down page corners and scribble in margins, it is best to keep me away from first editions.

On the jumbly shelves in my house I can find directions for replacing a broken pipe stem, a history of corncribs, a booklet of Spam recipes, a 1925 copy of *Animal Heroes of the Great War* (mostly dogs but some camels); dictionaries of slang, dialect and regional English; a pile of Little Blue Books (none are blue) from the 1920s featuring titles like *How to Be a Gate-Crasher* and *Character Reading From the Face.* One of these, *Curiosities of Language,* treats us to the tortured orthography our grandparents thought hilarious:

> There was a young man, a Colonel,
> Who walked in the breezes volonel;
> He strolled in the aisles,
> Of the wooded maisles,
> And, returning, read in his jolonel.

This digging involves more than books. I need to know which mushrooms smell like maraschino cherries and which like dead rats, to note that a magpie in flight briefly resembles a wooden spoon, to recognize vertically trapped suppressed lee-wave clouds; so much of this research is concerned with four-dimensional observation and notation. These jottings go into cheap paper-covered notebooks that I keep in a desultory fashion, more often onto the backs of envelopes and the margins of newspapers, from there onto the floor of the truck or onto the stair landing atop a stack of faxes and bills.

The need to know has taken me from coal mines to fire towers, to hillsides studded with agate, to a beached whale skeleton, to the sunny side of an iceberg, to museums of canoes and of windmills, to death masks with eyelashes stuck in the plaster, to shipyards and log yards, old military forts, wildfires and graffiti'd rocks, to rough water and rusty shipwrecks, to petroglyphs and prospectors' diggings, to collapsed cotton gins, down into the caldera of an extinct volcano and, once or thrice in the middle distance, in view of a snouty twister.

I listen attentively in bars and cafés, while standing in line at the checkout counter, noting particular pronunciations and the rhythms of regional speech, vivid turns of speech and the duller talk of everyday life. In Melbourne I paid money into the hand of a sidewalk poetry reciter to hear "The Spell of the Yukon," in London listened to a cabby's story of his psychopath brother in Paris, on a trans-Pacific flight heard from a New Zealand engineer the peculiarities of building a pipeline across New Guinea.

The grand digging grounds are still the secondhand book-shops. Every trip ends with boxes of books shipped back, dusty old manuals on the hide business or directions for the dances of Texas with footprints and dotted lines reeling across the pages. But bookstores are changing. Recently I rattled the latch of a favorite in Denver before I saw the sign announcing that it was forever closed, but the inventory could be "accessed" on the Internet. Another dealer, a specialist in local histories, operated from his living room for years and put out an interesting catalogue from time to time. Both the catalogue and a visit to his bookshelves are things of the past, rendered obsolete by chilly cyber-lists.

I rarely use the Internet for research, as I find the process cumbersome and detestable. The information gained is often untrustworthy and couched in execrable prose. It is unpleasant to sit in front of a twitching screen suffering assault by virus, power outage, sluggish searches, system crashes, the lack of direct human discourse, all in an atmosphere of scam and hustle.

Nor do I do much library research these days, though once I haunted the stacks. Libraries have changed. They are no longer quiet but rather noisy places where people gather to exchange murder mysteries. In bad weather homeless folk exuding pungent odors doze at the reading tables. One stands in line to use computers, not a few down for the count, most with smeared and filthy screens, running on creaky software.

I mourn the loss of the old card catalogues, not because I'm a Luddite, but because the oaken trays of yesteryear offered the researcher an element of random utility and felicitous surprise through encounters with adjacent cards: information by chance that is different in kind from the computer's ramified but rigid order.

This country swims in fascinating pamphlets. In a New Mexico greasy spoon I pick up a flyer that takes St. Paul sharply to task on the subjects of hair style, clothing and women. ("Shorts, miniskirts, halters, bikinis, etc., are all OK. You don't have to listen to Paul. . . . God wants women to look nice and be in style with the times. As far as men, Jesus had long hair. Paul must have been a religious fanatic.") A hundred miles later I read a narrow sheet with advice on how to behave in the presence of a mountain lion. ("Do not make direct eye contact. . . . Try to appear as big as possible.")

Food and regional dishes are important research subjects.

Some you can order in restaurants, but others exist only in out-of-print cookbooks and must be prepared at home, like a duck roasted inside a watermelon, a dish called Angel in a Cradle, or another called the Atlanta Special, which sounds like a train, although the ingredient list begins, "1 beaver (8 to 10 pounds)."

I like to drive in the West, making a slow drift over caliche and gravel roads, volume cranked up and listening to music (this, too, is research), usually regional subtexts of alternative genres. But two that I never tire of hearing are Glenn Ohrlin singing "Barnacle Bill, the Sailor," in his two-tone voice, and the good ol' boy Texas country-and-western yodeler Don Walser with the Kronos string quartet, sliding a heartaching "Rose Marie" straight at me.

The truck wanders around intersecting roads as tangled as fishing line. At times topographic maps, compass bearings or keeping the sun at my shoulder are better direction guides than signs, usually nonexistent or bullet-blasted into unreadability. The rules of road drift are simple: Always take a branching side route, stop often, get out and listen, walk around, see what you see. And what you see are signs, not direction signs but the others, the personal messages. We live in a world of signs.

I am amazed when people mourn the loss of the Burma Shave jingles. Better stuff is all around us, in public restrooms, in phone booths, on rocks, stapled to telephone poles, struck on lawns. I remember a large billboard that stood for many years on a back-country road in Colorado. The community used it as a kind of enormous greeting card, welcoming home a son on leave from the Navy, congratulating a child on her fifth birthday, inviting neighbors to a party.

The signs of urban panhandlers seem to indicate that many of them took creative-writing courses. These messages are always printed in neat capital letters: "WILL KILL FOR FOOD," "BIG DUMB UGLY BUM NEEDS YOUR HELP," "MY MOTHER LOVED ME BUT NOW SHE'S GONE."

The digging is never done because the shovel scrapes at life itself. It is not possible to get it all, or even very much of it, but I gather what I can of the rough, tumbling crowd, the lone walkers and the voluble talkers, the high lonesome singers, the messages people write and leave for me to read.

If You Invent the Story, You're the First to See How It Ends

~

Roxana Robinson

One afternoon I was driving along the narrow dirt road on which I live. Ahead of me was a small red car with two people in the front seat. You can't go very fast on a dirt road, so we were poking along. As we did, I began to watch the car in front of me. The driver was a middle-aged man wearing glasses, and beside him sat a woman with long, wavy blond hair.

I could see the man's face because he kept turning and talking to the woman, but I couldn't see her face because she never turned to look at him or answer.

As we drove along, the man turned again and again, talking to the woman. He had thinning hair and a kindly face. Everything about him, his gestures, the way he spoke, seemed friendly and affectionate: he leaned toward her, he smiled. But she sat without movement or response, staring straight ahead. She never once looked in his direction, and I wondered why.

I supposed of course that they were fighting. The long blond hair suggested someone who was beautiful, or anyway someone who invited admiration and was used to it. I thought she might be arrogant and imperious, coldhearted, the way a beautiful woman, spoiled by her beauty, can be. I thought that the man might be her husband, or her lover, and that he was pleading with her. I thought she was turning cold to him; perhaps she was ending things completely, and he was trying to win her back. I felt sorry for the man, who was trying so hard to reach her, to save things.

We both slowed down to cross a little stone bridge, and once past it, on the straight, he turned again to her. I wondered then if I'd gotten it wrong. The man was definitely middle-aged, and the woman's long, thick blond hair suggested youth. Perhaps the man was not her husband but her father.

Perhaps he was pleading with her about something else: maybe about her behavior toward her mother, for example, or her grades or her attitude in school. Maybe she was sitting sullenly still, not heartlessly. Or maybe it was something else: maybe she was not stony-faced and implacable or sullen, but miserable. Maybe she was weeping and unable to look at her father. Perhaps he was trying to comfort her for a young man's cruelty or some other terrible teenage disappointment.

I watched him closely, trying to decipher the story. The man turned to her, smiling, tilting his head coaxingly. She still did not look at him. I felt sympathy for the man, making such a tender and dedicated effort; and sympathy for the woman, locked in such a paralyzed and miserable state.

We reached the stop sign at the end of Mount Holly Road, and the man turned once more to the blond woman.

This time, at last, she turned toward him. She leaned over and licked his nose. She was a golden retriever.

The reason for this story is to give you some idea of what it's like to be a writer. How odd an occupation it is, how unpredictable and how humbling.

I'm often asked when I started writing. But the important question is not when do writers start, but why.

My own reasons for writing, for setting down the story, are to a large extent selfish. With each story—and by story I mean anything I write—I am trying simply to work something out for myself. You, the reader, play no part here: this is a private matter.

I write about the things that trouble me. I write about the things that disturb me, the things that won't let me alone, the things that are eating slowly into my brain at three in the morning, the things that unbalance my world. Sometimes these are things I've said or done; sometimes they're things I've heard about or seen. Sometimes they're only sentences, sometimes scenes, sometimes complete narratives. I carry these things around inside my head until I'm compelled to write them down to get rid of them. I sit down and begin.

I know where I'm going: I'm going toward that troubling moment, the unforgivable statement, the irreversible act that has been gnawing at me. That's what's coming at the end of the story, and my task is to write my way to that moment in a way that explains it completely to me. If I can set down these moments and make them whole within a context that explains the scene and characters whose behavior I can forgive, then the moments become comprehensible to me. When I understand them, they lose their power to disturb. Then the anxieties subside and let me sleep. I really write to free myself.

As you can tell from the golden retriever, what I find most persistently interesting and compelling are stories about families. The family is at the heart of our emotional lives. It's where the heat is, the source of our most powerful feelings.

Family connections—between parent and child, brother and sister, husband and wife—form the strongest bonds we will ever know. These are the people who can make us happier, and angrier, than anyone else on earth. And these connections are indestructible: you might reject your family members, you might refuse to see them ever again, but they will still be your family. You will always be a part of them, whether you choose to be or not. The family will always have formed you. That was your childhood, no matter what you wish.

Your feelings for your family will be powerful ones, even if you deny them. If you were to decide, at twenty, never to speak to your mother again, and if you didn't see your mother for forty years, she would still be your mother. She would still have formed crucial parts of your sensibility.

When you do see her forty years later, by accident, as you surely will, when you catch a glimpse of her at someone's funeral, standing unevenly on the sloping lawn of the cemetery, grimly holding her pocketbook in the way you so well remember; or if you finally steel yourself and deliberately pay her a visit, in that first moment, as she opens the door and stands motionless in the doorway, silent, as though she doesn't know you. Then at that moment all those feelings that made you long ago decide never to see her again will come boiling up inside you.

You can't escape: those early feelings run at full spate for your entire lifetime, even if you can't bear to think of them.

Even if you refuse to acknowledge them, they are still there, pulsing and coursing below the surface, in silence and darkness, like an underground river. They govern our surface lives more than we think, and at any moment they may rise up from the darkness into full view, where they will explode into foam and torrents.

Perhaps the best thing about the family is that all of the emotions within it depend upon love, which is the most powerful. All the darker ones—rage and hatred and resentment—result from the absence of love, or its withholding; but love is the prime mover. And the fact that love is a part of any emotional equation means that the emotional life is always fluid, always in a state of flux: forty years of resentment can be ended, erased completely, if the love is at last forthcoming.

Of course if love has been withheld for forty years, the chances of its being freely given now are slim. It's just as likely that your father will turn his face to the wall and die, rather than speak to you at last. But something transforming might happen. He might speak. Or you might at last understand why he can't, and forgive him. You might feel the love you've missed, even if he cannot.

As a subject, the family is inexhaustible. Tolstoy is mistaken: all happy families are not alike. In fact no two families are alike, happy or unhappy. Every family, like every fingerprint, has its own unique pattern, its own set of conflicts and beliefs and alliances. They're formed by all sorts of things—class, education, language and physical heredity, just for starters; and growing up within our own family, we assume that our experience and its behavior is the norm.

We assume that a father always gets up first on Sunday

morning and comes down in his dressing gown to make everyone breakfast. Or that a mother never takes the animals to the vet because she throws up at the smell. Or that during fights a mother always retreats into the bedroom closet and holds the door shut. These things, you assume, are given, they are fixed.

Larger issues—America as a democratic institution, whether we should support capital punishment—these are in the arena of public discussion. You know people have a variety of attitudes toward them. You know how your fiancé feels about those things because you've talked about them. You discover the other, more important things later. You don't find out about other families' patterns until you've married into them, and then you find yourself arguing, indignantly, with utter disbelief about who should cook breakfast on Sundays, or who should take the dog for his shots, or whether you should be shouting out these views from inside the bedroom closet.

All this beauty and fury makes the family a rich literary source. Much of our greatest fiction comes from conflicts within it: look at *Oedipus Rex*, *King Lear*, *Anna Karenina*, *The Sound and the Fury*, *To the Lighthouse*, the Rabbit quartet. These works reveal us to ourselves, and it seems to me that this is who we are: we're people driven, damaged and tortured; we're people elated, sustained and nourished, all by the powerful, devastating, inescapable bonds within the family.

As the golden retriever story reveals, I love all the issues, large and small, comic and tragic. I love hearing about them, I love thinking about them, and I even love struggling with the dark ones, late at night. They are endlessly interesting to me and endlessly surprising.

Thinking about these endless, intricate, wonderful stories seems to be the task that's set for me, and I'm grateful for it. The stories are all around me. All I want is the opportunity to discover, ponder and absorb them, then to set them down. I want to get them exactly right. When I think I've succeeded at that, then I feel I have accomplished something.

And this is where you, the reader, come in. For only you will know for certain if I have.

Once Upon a Time, Literature. Now What?

James Salter

The first great task in life, by far the most important one, the one on which everything else depends, can be described in three words. Very simply, it is learning to speak. Language—whatever language, English, Swahili, Japanese—is the requisite for the human condition. Without it there is nothing. There is the beauty of the world and the beauty of existence, or the sorrow if you like, but without language they are inexpressible.

Animals are our companions, but they cannot, in any comparable sense, speak. They do not have, even the most majestic or intelligent of them—whales, elephants, lions—a God. In whatever form, our apprehension and worship of God is entirely dependent on language: prayers, sermons, hymns, the Bible or other text. Without language God might exist but could not be described.

In the richness of language, its grace, breadth, dexterity, lies its power. To speak with clarity, brevity and wit is like holding a lightning rod. We are drawn to people who know things and are able to express them: Dr. Johnson, Shakespeare. Language like theirs sets the tone, the language of poets, of heroes. A certain level of life, an impregnable level, belongs to them.

There is not just one language, however. There are two, the spoken and the written. The spoken is like breath, effortless and at hand. The written is another matter. Learning to read and write is a difficult business, the second portal. Once through it, you are into the open, as it were, the endless vistas. The *biblios* is there for you. I made up the word. It means library, archive, vast collection. A made-up word here or there is not much. Shakespeare made up nearly one in twelve of the more than twenty thousand he used over all; at least no previous use of them is known. The King James Bible by comparison contains only some eight thousand different words.

In the biblios are books, manuscripts, newspapers, printouts of Web sites, letters, all manner of things. The books are the most important. It is from reading them that one gets the urge to be a writer, or so it used to be. The first book that I believe I read in its entirety and on my own was *All Quiet on the Western Front.* I can't say that reading it made me want to be a writer, or that I became an avid reader, but the confidence and simplicity of the prose made a deep impression.

I remember lines from it even today. Sixty years have passed. I later heard that Erich Maria Remarque had been the editor of a German fashion magazine and decided to quit his job and write a novel. You're crazy, they told him. But the issues of *Die Dame,* or whatever it was, the lunches and dinners and perhaps the models have all disappeared, but not the novel.

I understood, of course—it was dogma—that a true education was based on being well read, and for ten years or more I read all I could. These were wonderful years of voyage, discovery and self-esteem. I would never catch up with those for whom reading was a passion, but I had climbed high.

I read less now. Perhaps it's loss of appetite. I read fewer books—reading is a pleasure, and I'm supposed to be working—but I am not less interested in them. They have not moved from their central position in my life.

At one time I thought frequently about death. It was when I was barely thirty and said to myself, "More than a third of your life is gone!" Now, for a different reason, I have started to think about it again. I like the image of the ancients, the crossing of a river. Sometimes I think of what, when the time comes, I might want to have with me. I can go without an expensive watch, without money or clothes, without a toothbrush, without having shaved, but can I go without certain books and, more than books, things I have written, not necessarily published?

The other day I was reading an essay by Deborah Eisenberg, a writer I have never met, called "Resistance." Very well written, it brought to mind the lucidity and aplomb of Virginia Woolf. The subject of the essay was writing, and I came, midway, to a sentence that ended, "part of the same disaster that has placed virtually every demanding or complex literary experience beyond our culture's confines."

I stopped there. I was unable to go on until I had sorted out a number of thoughts that had been aroused. "The same disaster. . . ." It brought to mind Nikos Kazantzakis's observation that the Apollonian crust of the world had, in modern times, been broken. From somewhere beneath, the Dionysian had poured forth.

Then the last words of the sentence, "our culture's confines." There came the persistent question: What is culture and what has become of ours? The dictionary definition is vague, "the sum total of the attainments and learned behavior patterns of any specific period or people." Let me list instead what I consider the components. I would say culture is language, art, history and customs.

We know that what is called popular culture has overwhelmed high culture with consequences not yet fully realized. Pop culture's patrons, youth and a large number of those who were formerly young, have rewarded it with immense riches, advancing it further. Junk like George Lucas's *Star Wars* trilogy or quintet becomes the most consuming and widely discussed, sometimes in terms appropriate to masterworks, artistic endeavor. Are we witnessing a mere collapse of taste or the actual genesis of a new myth worthy of replacing the outdated Trojan War or of standing beside it? As with the glorious stock boom, age-old standards of value are henceforth cast aside.

We seem to have seen it already, those of us old enough to remember. It was then called *Flash Gordon*, with similar location and cast, a cruel and omnipotent villain, a beautiful girlfriend of the hero, a wise old counselor, futuristic weapons, spacecraft, distant planets, air armadas. It was only a comic strip then. Schoolboys followed it. In its new form it has become a mine for academics and for those undergraduate courses called film studies.

When I wrote movies, which I did for about fifteen years, thinking of Graham Greene and John Steinbeck, who were writers as well as film writers, I was for a long time unaware of what it all looks like viewed from above, a writer as someone who must be employed preliminary to the real work. And the balance between what I wrote and what was made was low, about four scripts written for each one shot, with the best work ending up in the trash. The waste was depressing and also the venal stench that is the perfume of the business. Still, the ascendance of movies is irreversible.

The life-giving novel, like the theater, despite occasional flare-ups, belongs in the past. There is a limited audience. Céline, in an interview in *The Paris Review*, said, "Novels are something like lace . . . an art that went out with the convent." Literature is not dead—students still read Dostoyevsky and Whitman—but it has lost its eminence. The tide is turning against it.

I have heard figures of authority say that the Beatles' songs will be played three hundred years from now, and that Richard Wagner, were he alive today, would be a movie director. Can these things be true? We are not in a position to know, nor can we even be sure which way the great ship is turning.

Only a few things seem certain. The future, as Don DeLillo put it, belongs to crowds. The megacities, like cancer, have appeared with their great extremes of poverty and wealth, their isolation from what was called the natural world with its rivers, forests, silent dawns and nights. The new populations will live in hives of concrete on a diet of film, television and the Internet. We are what we eat. We are also what we see and hear. And we are in the midst of our one and only life.

More and more I am aware of people who are successful in every visible way and who have no sensitivity to art, no interest in history, and are essentially indifferent to language. It's hard to imagine that anything in their experience other than the birth of a child might elicit from them the word *transcendent*; ecstasy for them has a purely physical meaning, and yet they are happy. Culture is not necessary for them although they like to keep up with movies and music and perhaps the occasional best-seller. Is culture essential, then? Not pop culture but something higher, something that may endure?

Perhaps not. Whether humankind or nations advance or decline is a matter of unimportance to the planets and what lies beyond. If civilizations reach a new zenith or if they founder is a concern only to us and not really much of a concern since individually we can do so little about it.

At the same time it is frightening to think of a glib, soulless, pop culture world. There is the urge toward things that are not meaningless, that will not vanish completely without leaving the slightest ripple. The corollary to this is the desire to be connected to the life that has gone before, to stand in the ancient places, to hear the undying stories. Art is the real history of nations, it has been said. What we call literature, which is really only writing that never stops being read, is part of this. When it relinquishes its place, what is there to substitute for it?

It was Edwin Arlington Robinson, I think, who when he lay dying asked that his bed be taken out beneath the stars. That's the idea, anyway, not to breathe your last looking at some TV sitcom, but to die in the presence of great things, those riches—the greatest of all riches, in fact—that can be in the reach of anyone.

Starting with a Tree
and Finally Getting to
the Death of a Brother

~

William Saroyan

How do you write? My answer is that I start with the trees and keep right on straight ahead.

I start with these companions of this place, each fixed into the soil of where it is, and sometimes the rock or rocks, and very little else, and after that the going is not only easy, it is very nearly rollicking, for the tree is a thing of great attachments, and it puts forth all manner of leaves, abundantly, and each leaf is the same, but not precisely so, so that noticing this repetitious imprecision leads to everything else, especially life, especially speculation and especially the last act of life, the unknown abandonment of tree, branch, twig, leaf, bud, flower, fruit and self.

How do you die, write, live, sicken, heal, despair, rejoice? You are lucky if you don't start at the end, at abstraction. If you start at the beginning, at the specific, the seen, the real, and if you are a writer, you cannot permit yourself to be limited, although in your art, in your writing, in your tiny microscopic making, you have got to impose limits, after all, or you will be able to make nothing. You start with the visible but really impossible to hold: that gift that is swiftly made commonplace by familiarity, that demonstration of the infinitude of sameness, of flame, of color, of structure, of design, of mass, of movement.

What a loveliness a fire in a fireplace is to the man sitting there watching and listening, and what sweet whisperings of all manner of language come from the wood being consumed by the fire. In fire we may answer the question of life and art, how you die, do, live.

I have a short story entitled "The Broken Wheel" from my earliest days, and I remember that when I was just beginning to write the story, I kept asking myself: "What's going on? Why are you writing about the old English walnut tree in the backyard of the rickety frame house at 2226 San Benito Avenue in Fresno, and about the two barns stuck together, and about the cactus plant, and the grass, and the creosote bushes in the empty lot adjoining that house?"

You didn't know the name of that scented plant, that stinking plant, stinking of something like kerosene, which years later you came upon by accident out by the Southern Pacific Railroad tracks, north from the center of town, and getting a whiff of the strong smell, forgotten for thirty or forty years. You whooped with joy, with restoration of youth and confusion and joy and joy again and again: so this is what the creosote bush is, then, about which I have read a dozen or more times in twenty or thirty years and never knew it was our own bush in the empty lot where we played peewee, horse, tin-can hockey, soccer, baseball, football and an assortment of invented, improvised games.

There is no how to it, no how do you write, no how do

you live, how do you die. If there were, nothing would live in the deep and very delicate chain of life. It is the doing that makes for continuance. It is not the knowing of how the doing is done.

The dancer may try to put into choreographic language, symbols and signs of his muscle and skill, so that others may dance that way again; but it doesn't seem to work. Others do not dance that way. They study and study the choreographic treasure of instruction and storage, but it doesn't work.

He who dances danced, he who saw him dance, she who saw her dance, he who danced with her, and watched with him, and studied and remembered what had been seen, he and she and they, dancing and dancing to the manuscript of instruction: they dance, but it isn't the same. Perhaps it is better, even, or might become better; but it is not the same. There is always only one of each, always, and two may be desirable but it is impossible. There is a different breath in every breather.

A writer writes, and if he begins by remembering a tree in the backyard, that is solely to permit him gradually to reach the piano in the parlor upon which rests the photograph of the kid brother killed in the war. And the writer, nine or ten years old at the time, can notice that his mother is crying at the loss of the kid brother, who, if the truth is told, was nothing much more than any kid brother, a brat, a kind of continuous nuisance, and yet death had made him the darling of the family heart.

And so I wrote it, starting with the old English walnut tree with every year literally thousands of the magnificent hard fruit, which, when you removed the black casing, which dried and could be made to crumble away to the grooved shell, which then you could break with a hammer and then behold as a design of intricate engineering, of art, of construction, the hardwood slick and light brown in its convolutions in which the meat of the nut, as it is called, had ripened to a substance with the most subtle and satisfying flavor implanted into anything that creatures including human beings and small boys, like Henry and Willie, as my brother and I were referred to by other members of the family and neighborhood, and still are, thank God, could remove from the shell and put into the mouth and taste and chew and swallow and never suspect that indeed that is how we do, how we live, how we die, how we write, how we read.

The story was published in late 1933 in a weekly English-language newspaper of the Armenians in Boston called *Hairenik*, which means Homeland, and by Edward J. O'Brien of the famous *Best Short Stories of America*, an annual book he had founded in 1915. This good man chose the story for his book in 1933, and I saw it and read it and thought about it, about what I had done, and I thought about the name of the writer of the story, which was Sirak Goryan, not William Saroyan, because I had wanted the writer to be altogether Armenian, or so I am able now to say, for Sirak is a kind of Old Testament name taken into the Armenian family, and Goryan, meaning lion cub, I had heard somewhere was the name of an Armenian writer of the twelfth century who was not ecclesiastical in his writing when everybody else was.

Goryan wrote about the people, he wrote about the world, he did not write about the angels and heaven. And by the time "The Broken Wheel" came out in *Best Short Stories of America*, I had finished writing all of the twenty-six stories in *The Daring Young Man on the Flying Trapeze and Other Stories*, by William Saroyan, written and offered to

Whit Burnett and his wife, Martha Foley, editors of *Story* magazine, subsidized somewhat by Random House and its founder, that jolly fellow of television's *What's My Line*, Bennett Cerf.

The writing of that story at the age of twenty-five seemed to inform me that I had served my apprenticeship and could now see to the continuation of my career. A few days before Christmas my mother, Takoohi, was visited by her famous and rich kid brother, Aram of Bitlis, and he soon ordered me out of her house because I was a fraud and a parasite, and my theory of being a writer was, at best, pathetic and at worst damned ruthless.

I went down the stairs of the second floor flat at number 348 Carl Street in San Francisco and walked from around eight to midnight, at which time I went home and went to bed. I knew that I had finally written a good story, and that writing would always be my first if not indeed my only calling, but I couldn't disagree too much with Aram of Bitlis. I agreed with him entirely that I must make my own way.

Only three or four days after this Armenian household scene a short note came to me from *Story* saying that I would soon receive a check for $15, in payment for "The Daring Young Man on the Flying Trapeze," signed by Martha Foley. I replied instantly that starting on January 1, 1934, I would send *Story* magazine a brand-new short story every day for the entire month.

I don't believe anybody has needed to understand my purpose in doing this: quite simply, this was a rhetorical piece of precognition, and the question implicit in it was this: Suppose there is a new writer with unmistakable talent, so what? For of course it must be understood that for ten long years I had been sending stories to editors and had been getting them back with rejection slips.

Now, had "The Daring Young Man on the Flying Trapeze" come back from *Story* with a rejection slip, or even a short not unfriendly note, I am obliged to make known that I absolutely would not have given up writing, for I had decided that if that was to be the case, I would go on working Saturdays at the Fior D'Italia stand in the Crystal Palace Market, as I had been lately working, from six in the morning to eleven o'clock at night for five silver dollars. Now, though, with the acceptance of the story, I acquired both the best possible option as well as the responsibility and the right to ask the rhetorical question that I had put into the form of an announcement that was bound to be considered a piece of silly bragging on the part of a desperate unpublished writer: "I'm a writer."

I had absolutely no doubt in my heart or mind that I could indeed write a short story a day for thirty-one days, but it was understandable that for the first eleven or twelve days of this business I had doubts about how Martha Foley and Whit Burnett were taking the performance. One day came a telegram saying: "Stories are arriving. Don't stop." In all I sent the husband-and-wife team perhaps as many as thirty-six stories in January 1934, and I remember that twice I wrote and mailed two stories, and one day wrote and mailed three. I wanted to. It was as simple as that.

And so there was Sirak Goryan, and there was William Saroyan, and they were one and the same, although Edward J. O'Brien informed his friends Whit Burnett and Martha Foley that in his opinion he had the better of the two new Armenian writers, and the editors of *Story* magazine responded that he was mistaken, for their Armenian writer had sent them a short story a day for the entire month of January 1934, and sometimes he had sent two brand-new short stories in one day, and once he sent three.

How do you write? You write, man, you write, that's how, and you do it the way the old English walnut tree puts forth leaf and fruit every year by the thousands. And so, feeling a little guilty for perhaps having deceived somebody, I finally wrote to Edward J. O'Brien and told him that Sirak Goryan was William Saroyan, and a year or two later we met and became good friends.

If you practice an art faithfully, it will make you wise, and most writers can use a little wising up.

The last manuscript of the American author William Saroyan (1908–81), which is being edited for publication, is excerpted here with permission of the trustees of Stanford University.

Opting for Invention over the Injury of Invasion

Carol Shields

One day I ran into an acquaintance at a shopping mall. She had just bought herself a beautiful new spruce-green nightgown, and she opened her bag an inch or two, so I might admire it.

"And now," she said, "I must rush off to buy some matching candles." I must have looked bewildered because she immediately explained, "Oh, I have candles to match all my nightgowns."

I was in the midst of a novel at the time, as I usually am, and I couldn't resist putting in this particular report from the Frontier of Real Life. I relish such curious glimpses into people's lives, flashes of uniqueness that reveal, in a blink of the eye, their extraordinary otherness.

But months later, when I came to read the proofs for the novel, I took the candles-and-nightgown reference out. My friend would be sure to read the book, and certainly she would recognize herself, since she must be the only person in the Western Hemisphere who carries color coordination to this extreme. The excision cost me a sigh of regret. But it preserved our acquaintance, and perhaps avoided a storm of self-consciousness on her part. For I am convinced that no one wants to make an appearance in someone else's fiction, whether in the guise of a slightly demented shopper or equipped with heroic raiment.

Perhaps this reluctance to be expropriated has its roots in the old legend about the camera stealing the souls of its subjects. But it is more likely to be, for me at least, an issue of privacy and the casual violation of another person's integrity, not to mention the possibility of lawsuits, parents suing their children or children suing a parent. Whether court actions succeed or fail, whether time will or won't erase an injury of invasion, it is hard to imagine there will ever be a scene of forgiveness between writer and victim and a return to normal relations.

Is it worth it? Every novelist will reply differently.

I made up my mind at the beginning of my writing life not to write about my family and friends, since I want them to remain my family and friends. Others, it seems, have come to a similar conclusion. The novelist Robertson Davies was once asked why he had waited until age sixty before writing his marvelous *Deptford Trilogy*. There was a long pause, and then he replied, haltingly, "Well, certain people died, you see."

Novelists inevitably arrive at a recipe for their work: so many parts observation and experience, combined with so many degrees of commitment to imagination. Stir well in a projected or real universe. Hope for a reader who understands what fiction really is and a critic who resists tying fictional gestures to autobiography.

Novelists tend to be clumsy with the question of where their material comes from. They shrug and blow out their cheeks in the French manner, dismissive, skeptical, unwilling to be caught out.

Well, yes, it is true I spent a winter in Algeria, true enough that I met an exiled Korean artist while there and true indeed that we traveled together in an old Ford station wagon to Rabat, and, yes, his wife really was a New Yorker, a Quaker, a poet bearing a superficial resemblance to Madame X. But all the rest is pure fabrication.

Where do you get your ideas?

My ideas? Well. Hmmmm. Which ideas would you be referring to?

Where does your material originate? Your characters? The narrative arc you employ?

This is a question contemporary novelists are often asked, and one they rightly suspect is a trap. Do you draw on real events, real people, real situations?

Hardly anyone is foolish enough to say yes, that novels are no more than a surface reworking of a private experience. The divorcing statement that introduces most fictions is both a legal dodge and a self-assertion, reminding both the author and the public of the role of imagination.

There is the standard: "This book is a work of fiction, and therefore names, characters, places and incidents are products of the author's imagination. Any resemblance to actual events or locales or persons, living or dead, is entirely coincidental."

Or, in a slyer, more ironic and perhaps more skeptical vein, we have Davies's disclaimer prefacing *The Salterton Trilogy*: "Readers who think that they can identify the creations of the author's fancy among their own acquaintance are paying the author an extravagant compliment, which he acknowledges with gratitude."

I've heard writers say that their friends wouldn't recognize themselves if they apprehended their image in the pages of a novel. Writerly paint would have blurred the outlines; writerly invention would have added enough ornamentation to conceal the true identity.

But readers are not so easily fooled as this, especially readers who have collided with novelists or even befriended them. They know they are in danger the minute they are admitted to a writer's life, and they read the published text with a magnifying lens in hand.

Could that be me, that fool dribbling coffee down his shirt front and babbling about the tyranny of life in the suburbs, about the betrayal of love? Yes, of course it's me.

During the twenty or so years I taught classes in creative writing, I never once encountered a student who didn't worry, at some level, that a friend or family member was going to be violated, punished or crucified in a piece of writing. (Mothers take an exceptionally heavy rap with younger students.) This fear persisted even among students whose work would stand scarcely any chance of ever being published. The concern was real, and often it afflicted young writers with classic writer's block before they'd written so much as a single word.

I always urged them to say what they had to say anyway, unshackled by any thought of personal response. They could revise afterward, I said, burying the real person by altering gender, race, the time frame, the geographical context. The choices were limitless. Write bravely, truly; revise with discretion, tact. This is easy enough to say, but I have come to understand exactly how difficult it is in the end to make the small and necessary sacrifices once words are committed to paper. There are times when changing even a name feels like a hideous compromise.

The inability of fiction to stare at itself goes back to the earliest novels of the eighteenth century and rises, I like to think, from the twinning of embarrassment and innocence. How does a writer confess that the printed offering is a tissue of imagination? The whole force of moral imperative rages against such a whimsical presentation: lying, inventing, daydreaming. In desperation early fiction writers supplied their narratives with implicitly understood framing devices like: This is a tale found in an old trunk. This is a story related to me by an ancient gentleman. This is a dream recorded by an angel.

We love fiction because it possesses the texture of the real. The characters in a novel resemble, more or less, ourselves. Fiction's dilemmas are similar to those we encounter every day, and there are novelists who do indeed write close to the autobiographical bone. As for the others, if they don't draw on their own experience, where on earth does it all come from?

The imaginative side of fiction writing is always hard to describe to nonwriters, those tunnels in the unconscious, those flitting responses to what might have been, what possibly could be.

There is a famous, perhaps whimsical story about the British writer John Buchan, who wrote dozens of successful adventure novels. At one point in his career he was determined to write a novel about the Canadian Arctic. This was some time before he arrived in Canada to serve as governor general, and he knew nothing in the way of background information. Fortunately, though, his son had just returned from spending a year there.

"Tell me ten facts about the Arctic," the elder Buchan demanded. The son began a list, but his father interrupted after just three facts had been delivered: "That's enough. That's plenty. I can manage with that."

The rest he could, and did, invent.

A Reluctant Muse
Embraces His Task,
and Everything Changes

~

Jane Smiley

The wholesale transformation of my writing life began, I suppose inevitably, with just a notion. I was beginning a new novel, a comic novel about horse racing, and I have to say I was inordinately pleased with it.

I had written a comic novel before, *Moo*, and I had certainly been my own best audience, sitting in my office, writing funny lines and pages and chapters, and laughing all the while. From time to time during *Moo* I would sashay out, a couple of pages in hand, and read something aloud, only to be greeted with well-meaning but blank stares. What in the world, who in the world, was I talking about?

In the end, of course, *Moo* found an audience, and several years after I so enjoyed myself, I started getting reviews and letters from others who also enjoyed themselves. But too late. I was writing *The All-True Travels and Adventures of Lidie Newton* by that time, and was no longer in the mood.

So. I had a new friend and a new novel. What could be

simpler than to bring the two together, that is, read the thing aloud to him chapter by chapter?

My friend, known as Jack, was a little perplexed. He was not a reader and had not read any of my books. He didn't know what his role was. Should he offer suggestions? Would he laugh in the right places? Would he get bored and fall asleep, especially since he knew nothing about horse racing?

What I didn't tell him was that the main point was my own enjoyment. His presence was merely to be the occasion for me to laugh at my own jokes. And actually he performed perfectly. All he did was laugh, nod, say mmmm, yes and thank you. Nary a suggestion, not to mention a criticism. And when I was in the middle of chapters, he would ask me when the next reading was going to be. I began pushing myself a bit, in order to finish enough to be able to invite him over.

It didn't take long for the transformation of my process to begin. From time to time I would write something and think not "Oh, I like that," but "Oh, Jack will like that." And I would laugh even harder, laughing for him, for me, and in anticipation of the pleasure of sharing with him.

Nor did it take long for him to orient himself in my aesthetic. The first two or three chapters he didn't quite understand or perfectly comprehend, but then I began to notice that just where I had intended a particular irony or a specific point, he would almost always grunt, chuckle, or murmur.

There were two ways of thinking about this. One was that my words were communicating clearly on levels of both sense and emotion. The other was that he and I were in sync. I chose both of the above.

After about 150 pages, maybe three months of reading, he offered a suggestion. I bridled but hid this. He was, after all, respectful and courteous in his manner. I listened. All he wanted was some clarification.

That's when I realized that he was the ideal audience even in this, that he always needed clarification in just those spots where I had been confused or careless. He was listening attentively enough to know when he didn't understand and to be able to distinguish what he didn't understand from what he did understand.

The fact that he only rarely requested clarification came to mean that he understood almost everything. What a relief that was. And then he offered a joke. All along I had been including jokes about animals in the novel, and when he told me this joke, I laughed so hard I threw the phone across the room. After I put it in and read it back to him, he corrected my wording and my timing just a little bit. The first time, I bridled at that, too.

There was the temptation, which I instantly gave in to, to depict our relationship, kaleidoscopically rearranged, in the novel and then read it back to him. These parts of the readings always aroused many hmmm's but no overt discussion or response. I understood that my right to my point of view was being honored, and that he understood that he was being shown what it meant to be observed in detail, one of the trials of intimacy with a writer.

We had a few discussions about the nature of observation: honesty, detachment and a measure of courage were required on the part of both the observer and the observed. These discussions showed me that I, too, was being observed, and that the truly interesting thing was not our particular observations of each other but the act of observation itself.

The fact that more than any of my other novels this one evolved in the making does not seem related to its being read aloud. But I often sat down to a new chapter and didn't have the first notion of what I was going to write, something I had never encountered, or perhaps I should say suffered, before. I often thought I knew exactly what was going to happen to a particular character, or how he or she would fit into the climax and the denouement, and I almost never did. But although I struggled with my imagination more than I ever had, what appeared on the computer screen after the struggle surprised and delighted me more than it ever had, and I was always eager to share it.

There was an improvisational exuberance that excited and entertained us both that, in retrospect, became the goal of each day's writing. I suspect that having a ready and non-judgmental audience gave me the freedom and comfort not to know what I was doing, to accept that a way of getting to the end that I did not understand would come to be under-stood once I got there.

Every other novel I had written had been a secret; that seemed to be inherent in novel writing. You went into your room one day, and some years later you presented the results of your private meditations, all neatened up and complete.

It was a good life for a secretive person, but I found it uncomfortable, a sort of double agentry in which who I was for a good part of every day was unavailable to my dearest companions and perhaps seemed to them to be just another form of commodity making. The process that for me pro-duced an evolution of thoughts, feelings, aesthetics and identity for them produced a book and an income. Including

Jack in my process made him party to the evolution, part of the evolution. We do not have even this benign secret between us.

Through this I came to see novel writing as more like running water through a hose than putting objects into a box. Because I spoke the novel as it came out, I was also more aware of how it went in: of the questions I asked people and their answers, of the things I observed and used, of what I eavesdropped upon and read and cooked together into the day's offering.

In his book *After Bakhtin*, David Lodge reflects upon the failure of much literary theory to grapple with the richness of the novel, and he locates this richness in the variety of voices that enter into the narrative, even when the author seems to have a strong voice of his or her own. This came to be my daily experience, a myriad of voices entering me and holding sway, sometimes for a whole chapter, sometimes for only a word.

I had always thought of novel writing as a social activity: the writer alone at a loud party in his office, entertaining a host of characters that no one else could see or hear. But this time I welcomed many more voices more actively, and they carried me, flowed through me to Jack, were returned to me in his attention and interest.

Of course, I suppose, two parties engaged in a comic novel will come to love each other, and we did, and the novel will grow more comic as the possibilities of love grow between them, as it did. We have discussed every piece I've written in the last year. When I told him this morning that I was going to write this piece on "the writing life," he said, "What are you going to write about?" I said I didn't know.

Then I said: "The writing life. I give you thirty seconds to come up with a word, any word." Thirty seconds later he said, "Love."

Yes, I thought, a novel is a spot where language, movement, feeling, and thought gel for a moment, through the agency of, let's say, a particular volunteer, but it is not an object or a possession. It is an act of love.

Directions: Write, Read, Rewrite. Repeat Steps 2 and 3 as Needed

Susan Sontag

Reading novels seems to me such a normal activity, while writing them is such an odd thing to do. . . . At least so I think until I remind myself how firmly the two are related. (No armored generalities here. Just a few remarks.)

First, because to write is to practice, with particular intensity and attentiveness, the art of reading. You write in order to read what you've written and see if it's OK and, since of course it never is, to rewrite it—once, twice, as many times as it takes to get it to be something you can bear to reread. You are your own first, maybe severest, reader. "To write is to sit in judgment on oneself," Ibsen inscribed on the flyleaf of one of his books. Hard to imagine writing without rereading.

But is what you've written straight off never all right? Sometimes even better than all right. And that only suggests, to this novelist at any rate, that with a closer look, or voicing aloud—that is, another reading—it might be better still. I'm not saying that the writer has to fret and sweat to produce something good. "What is written without effort is in general read without pleasure," said Dr. Johnson, and the maxim seems as remote from contemporary taste as its author. Surely, much that is written without effort gives a great deal of pleasure. No, the question is not the judgment of readers—who may well prefer a writer's more spontaneous, less elaborated work—but a sentiment of writers, those professionals of dissatisfaction. You think, If I can get it to this point the first go-around, without too much struggle, couldn't it be better still?

And though this, the rewriting—and the rereading—sound like effort, they are actually the most pleasurable parts of writing. Sometimes the only pleasurable parts. Setting out to write, if you have the idea of "literature" in your head, is formidable, intimidating. A plunge in an icy lake. Then comes the warm part: when you already have something to work with, upgrade, edit.

Let's say, it's a mess. But you have a chance to fix it. You try to be clearer. Or deeper. Or more eloquent. Or more eccentric. You try to be true to a world. You want the book to be more spacious, more authoritative. You want to winch yourself up from yourself. You want to winch the book out of your balky mind. As the statue is entombed in the block of marble, the novel is inside your head. You try to liberate it. You try to get this wretched stuff on the page closer to what you think your book should be—what you know, in your spasms of elation, it can be. You read the sentences over and over. Is this the book I'm writing? Is this all?

Or let's say, it's going well; for it does go well, sometimes. (If it didn't, some of the time, you'd go crazy.) There you are, and even if you are the slowest of scribes and the worst of touch typists, a trail of words is getting laid down, and you want to keep going; and then you reread it. Perhaps you don't dare to be satisfied, but at the same time you like what you've written. You find yourself taking pleasure—a reader's pleasure—in what's there on the page.

Writing is finally a series of permissions you give yourself to be expressive in certain ways. To invent. To leap. To fly. To fall. To find your own characteristic way of narrating and insisting; that is, to find your own inner freedom. To be strict without being too self-excoriating. Not stopping too often to reread. Allowing yourself, when you dare to think it's going well (or not too badly), simply to keep rowing along. No waiting for inspiration's shove.

Blind writers can never reread what they dictate. Perhaps this matters less for poets, who often do most of their writing in their head before setting anything down on paper. (Poets live by the ear much more than prose writers do.) And not being able to see doesn't mean that one doesn't make revisions. Don't we imagine that Milton's daughters, at the end of each day of the dictation of *Paradise Lost*, read it all back to their father aloud and then took down his corrections? But prose writers, who work in a lumberyard of words, can't hold it all in their heads. They need to see what they've written. Even those writers who seem most forthcoming, prolific, must feel this. (Thus Sartre announced, when he went blind, that his writing days were over.) Think of portly, venerable Henry James pacing up and down in a room in Lamb House composing *The Golden Bowl* aloud to a secretary. Leaving aside the difficulty of imagining how James's late prose could have been dictated at all, much less to the racket made by a Remington typewriter circa 1900, don't we assume that James reread what had been typed and was lavish with his corrections?

When I became, again, a cancer patient two years ago and had to break off work on the nearly finished *In America*, a kind friend in Los Angeles, knowing my despair and fear that now I'd never finish it, offered to take a leave from his job and come to New York and stay with me as long as needed, to take down my dictation of the rest of the novel. True, the first eight chapters were done (that is, rewritten and reread many times), and I'd begun the next-to-last chapter, and I did feel I had the arc of those last two chapters entirely in my head. And yet, and yet, I had to refuse his touching, generous offer. It wasn't just that I was already too befuddled by a drastic chemo cocktail and lots of painkillers to remember what I was planning to write. I had to be able to see what I wrote, not just hear it. I had to be able to reread.

Reading usually precedes writing. And the impulse to write is almost always fired by reading. Reading, the love of reading, is what makes you dream of becoming a writer. And long after you've become a writer, reading books others write—and rereading the beloved books of the past—constitutes an irresistible distraction from writing. Distraction. Consolation. Torment. And, yes, inspiration.

Of course, not all writers will admit this. I remember once saying something to V. S. Naipaul about a nineteenth-century English novel I loved, a very well-known novel that I assumed he, like everyone I knew who cared for literature, admired as I did. But no, he'd not read it, he said, and seeing the shadow of surprise on my face, added sternly, "Susan, I'm a writer, not a reader." Many writers who are no longer young claim, for various reasons, to read very little, indeed, to find reading and writing in some sense incompatible. Perhaps, for some writers, they are. It's not for me to judge. If the reason is anxiety about being influenced, then this seems to me a vain, shallow worry. If the reason is lack of time—there are only so many hours in the day, and those spent reading are evidently subtracted from those in which one could be writing—then this is an asceticism to which I don't aspire.

Losing yourself in a book, the old phrase, is not an idle fantasy but an addictive, model reality. Virginia Woolf famously said in a letter, "Sometimes I think heaven must be one continuous unexhausted reading." Surely the heavenly part is that—again, Woolf's words—"the state of reading consists in the complete elimination of the ego." Unfortunately, we never do lose the ego, any more than we can step over our own feet. But that disembodied rapture, reading, is trancelike enough to make us feel ego-less.

Like reading, rapturous reading, writing fiction—inhabiting other selves—feels like losing yourself, too.

Everybody likes to think now that writing is just a form of self-regard. Also called self-expression. As we're no longer supposed to be capable of authentically altruistic feelings, we're not supposed to be capable of writing about anyone but ourselves.

But that's not true. William Trevor speaks of the boldness of the nonautobiographical imagination. Why wouldn't you write to escape yourself as much as you might write to express yourself? It's far more interesting to write about others.

Needless to say, I lend bits of myself to all my characters. When, in *In America*, my immigrants from Poland reach

Southern California—they're just outside the village of Anaheim—in 1876, stroll out into the desert and succumb to a terrifying, transforming vision of emptiness, I was surely drawing on my own memory of childhood walks into the desert of southern Arizona—outside what was then a small town, Tucson—in the 1940s. In the first draft of that chapter, there were saguaros in the Southern California desert. By the third draft I had taken the saguaros out, reluctantly. (Alas, there aren't any saguaros west of the Colorado River.)

What I write about is other than me. As what I write is smarter than I am. Because I can rewrite it. My books know what I once knew—fitfully, intermittently. And getting the best words on the page does not seem any easier, even after so many years of writing. On the contrary.

Here is the great difference between reading and writing. Reading is a vocation, a skill, at which, with practice, you are bound to become more expert. What you accumulate as a writer are mostly uncertainties and anxieties.

All these feelings of inadequacy on the part of the writer—this writer, anyway—are predicated on the conviction that literature matters. *Matters* is surely too pale a word. That there are books that are "necessary," that is, books that, while reading them, you know you'll reread. Maybe more than once. Is there a greater privilege than to have a consciousness expanded by, filled with, pointed to literature?

Book of wisdom, exemplar of mental playfulness, dilator of sympathies, faithful recorder of a real world (not just the commotion inside one head), servant of history, advocate of contrary and defiant emotions . . . a novel that feels necessary can be, should be, most of these things.

As for whether there will continue to be readers who share this high notion of fiction, well, "there's no future to that question," as Duke Ellington replied when asked why he was to be found playing morning programs at the Apollo. Best just to keep rowing along.

An Odyssey That
Started with *Ulysses*

Scott Turow

A t the age of eighteen, after my freshman year in college, I worked as a mailman. This was merely a summer job. My life's calling, I had decided, was to be a novelist,
and late at night I was already toiling on my first novel.

One of the glories of postal employment in those days
was that once carriers learned their routes, they could
deliver the mail in far less than the five hours allotted.
By long-standing agreement—explained to me in a most
emphatic and furtive way by a colleague my first week—
mail carriers who finished early did not return to the post
office until the end of the day.

Since the public library was the only air-conditioned
public building, even in that affluent suburban town, I spent
my free time there. And inasmuch as I wanted to be a novelist, I decided to read James Joyce's *Ulysses*.

By then I had read Joyce's magnificent first novel, *Portrait
of the Artist as a Young Man*, and I wanted to be a novelist
just like him. In homage to Joyce's embroidery from the stuff

of the Greek myths, I'd called my first novel "Dithyramb," the name of a Bacchic dance whose relevance was entirely elusive, even then, to my story of two teenage runaways from Chicago who witness a murder.

As for *Ulysses*, even as a freshman I'd been taught that it was hands down the best novel ever written. The literary god T. S. Eliot had hailed the book in 1923 as "the most important expression" of its age. "If it is not a novel, that is simply because the novel is a form which will no longer serve," said Eliot, praising Joyce for being in advance of his time.

So for the next eight weeks I read the novel to end all novels for an hour and a half each afternoon at taxpayer expense. A number of things struck me about *Ulysses*. First, it was hard. When I finished, I was glad I'd read it, but I didn't mind that I'd been paid by the hour to do it.

I was also troubled that the library's single volume of *Ulysses* was there every day when I went for it, never checked out. It seemed that no one else in this well-to-do, highly educated community wanted to read the greatest novel ever written, at least not in the leisure hours of summer. I thought inevitably of the philosophical riddle with which schoolchildren were routinely teased in those days: If a tree falls in the forest and no one hears it, is there sound?

Thus began the questions that plagued me for years. Was *Ulysses* really a great work of literature, if almost no one read it for leisure, and if the few who dared found it so taxing? What did writers owe their audience? How easy were we supposed to make things for them? And what were we entitled to demand in return?

It was obvious that every writer, at least those who sought to publish, craved an audience. But on what terms?

The modernists, for example, did not aim to be read by everybody. Their attitudes were well expressed in Eliot's remarks about Joyce or in Ezra Pound's declaration "Artists are the antennae of the race, but the bullet-headed many will never learn to trust their great artists."

In the modernists' view the writer's job was to lead culture, to reinvent art constantly, thereby providing society with previously undiscovered insights. It did not matter if the bullet-headed didn't understand *Ulysses*, provided the few who could change culture did.

The radical democrat in my soul who was running amok in the '60s had a hard time buying this. Yet even I had to accept the modernists' formulation that artists must lead. But my view was more of an I-thou relationship: the artist offers a special vision that reframes experience in a way that, although intensely personal, reverberates deeply among us all.

To lead and arouse a universal audience seemed the writer's task, yet it was hardly clear to me how to do it. Following college I spent several years at the Creative Writing Center at Stanford University, first as a fellow and later as a lecturer. The center was roiled by intense factional rivalries that echoed much of my own turmoil.

A clutch of antirealists, self-conscious innovators, championed the views of John Hawkes, who had once declared, "I began to write fiction on the assumption that the true enemies of the novel were plot, character, setting and theme." The experimentalists reacted in horror when I contended that the ideal novel would be equally stirring to a bus driver and an English professor.

My ideas were much closer to those of my teacher, Wallace Stegner, a realist writer in the tradition of James and Dreiser, which had stressed an exacting representation of our experience in the everyday world. The realists eschewed Dickensian plot, since it depended on coincidence or the kind of odd or extreme behavior we don't commonly witness. Despite my affinities, I was tweaked by the experimentalists' complaints that the resulting literature was often static.

I dug through these issues in my own work, spending my years at Stanford writing a novel about a rent strike in Chicago. The book was steeped in the intricacies of real estate law, which explained in part why it, like "Dithyramb," went unpublished.

Nonetheless, writing the book had opened me to a previously unrecognized passion for the law. I startled everyone, even myself, by abandoning my academic career in favor of law school, vowing all the same to live on as a writer. By the time I graduated, I had published *One L*, a nonfiction account of my first year at law school. But I still yearned to be a novelist, even as law school had confirmed my attraction to the life of a working lawyer and, especially, to criminal law.

I was hired as a prosecutor in the United States Attorney's Office in Chicago. There I was astonished to find myself facing the same old questions about how to address an audience. The trial lawyer's job and the novelist's were, in some aspects, shockingly similar. Both involved the reconstruction of experience, usually through many voices, whether they were witnesses or characters. But there the paths deviated. In this arena the universal trumped; there were no prizes for being rarefied or ahead of the times. The trial lawyer who lost the audience also inevitably lost the case.

Engaging the jury was indispensable, and again and

again I received the same advice about how to do it: Tell them a good story. There were plenty of good stories told in the courtroom, vivid accounts of crimes witnessed or conspiracies joined. The jury hung in primal fascination, waiting to find out what happened next. And so did I.

Thus I suddenly saw my answer to the literary conundrum of expressing the unique for a universal audience: Tell them a good story. The practice of criminal law had set me to seething with potential themes: the fading gradations between ordinary fallibility and great evil; the mysterious passions that lead people to break the known rules; the mirage that the truth often becomes in the courtroom.

The decision to succumb to plot and to the tenacious emotional grip I felt in contemplating crime led me naturally to the mystery whose power as a storytelling form persisted despite its long-term residence in the low-rent precincts of critical esteem. I was certain that an audience's hunger to know what happened next could be abetted by some of the values of the traditional realist novel, especially psychological depth in the characters and a prose style that aimed for more than just dishing out plot.

Furthermore the supposedly timeworn conventions of genre writing seemed actually to offer an opportunity for innovation. Why not, for example, invert the traditional detective tale by having the investigator accused of the crime?

Thus was born *Presumed Innocent*. I worked on that book for eight years on the morning commuter train and was staggered by its subsequent emergence as a best-seller. My only goal had been finally to publish a novel. I didn't even like most best-sellers, which I deemed short on imagination.

I have, frankly, learned to enjoy all the rewards of best-sellerdom, but none more than the flat-out, juvenile thrill of entering so many lives. I love my readers with an affection that is second only to what I feel for my family and friends, and I would be delighted to please them with every new book.

But I am, all the same, desperate not to be captured by that audience. I have self-consciously avoided cloning *Presumed Innocent* (to the oft-stated disappointment of many), knowing self-imitation would violate the rules I set for myself to start. Art—or whatever it is I'm doing—begins with the maker, not the audience. Capitulating to established expectations means abandoning that obligation to lead and is likely to yield the larded stuff that too often oozes out of the Hollywood sausage grinder.

Graham Greene, probably this century's most admired writer of suspense fiction, remarked that all writers tend to be governed by "a ruling passion." I regard myself as blessed to have been able to discover mine.

Over time I've realized that the ideal novel that deeply stirs everyone will never be written. Even *Anna Karenina* grows tiresome for some readers. The only true transcendence is achieved by the entire family of writers—of artists—who, together, manage to move us all. As individuals we can only dig toward our ruling passions, uncover them and desperately hope, as we fall, to be heard.

Questions of Character: There's No Ego as Wounded as a Wounded Alter Ego

~

John Updike
(as Henry Bech)

O ne—not the only one—of the spiritual burdens of being a New Yorker is an undue reverence for the *New York Times*; when a minion of that sacrosanct rag approached this above-signed ancient penman and asked him to interview, not for the first time, a writer a tad less ancient but inconveniently resident hundreds of miles up the Atlantic Seaboard, I could not find it in my heart to say no. John Updike was the name of my designated victim, on the slender but penetrating excuse that he had chosen to perpetrate, in his impudence and ignorance, a book ostensibly about me—*Bech at Bay*, five tales full of fantastic details concerning the latter-day life of a Jewish-American prosist bearing my name.

My traducer's lonely aerie was not easy to locate, though

I had been there once before, on a similar journalistic errand. North of Boston, the landscape becomes a drab pudding of rocks and conifers, of abandoned factories and clapboarded shacks boasting (the houses wear wooden badges, with names and dates) of pre-Revolutionary origins. The nondescript burg that gives Updike refuge lies, along the tattered coast, one urban notch north of the second-rate port where Hawthorne once spun his dismal witcheries. Even in 1835, as I recall, Hawthorne felt that the good times, the majestic times, had gone by. And indeed today's wintry air savored of the mellowly bygone, of once-vital cultural impulses now subsided into a wide spatter of mock-Georgian educational institutions and a quaint liberalism that gives Massachusetts its all-Democrat representation in Congress.

Along a winding road that bisects a girls' college, past an iron fence that once stood guard before the summer residence of Henry Clay Frick, my nervous limo driver and I went; we traveled (if I may, in so self-reflective a piece, quote from my earlier account) "across some railroad tracks to what I presumed was the wrong side, where, after a few divagations into the driveways of indignant gentry, we eventually came upon the author, looking as elderly and vexed as his neighbors." Not quite "vexed" this time, perhaps—his step more hesitant, his white hair skimpier, Updike greeted me with a fraternal cordiality that I found, frankly, offensive. Though he lives, in the manner of suburban princelings, surrounded by foliating excrescences, I did not beat about the bush. Pulling out my Zippo-size tape recorder, I asked him:

Q. How could you have done this to me?

A. This further book of your uproarious adventures? I love you, Henry—isn't that reason enough? You are the person I, once a woeful country boy, wanted to be: a New York writer, up to his ears in toxic fumes. But I came to the metropolis, inhaled, and fled. What remains of that ignominious episode are the words *New York* on my elder son's birth certificate, and you. You have stayed the course. I envy you. I envy you your city banter, your zaftig women, your dignified ennui, your underground ability to tell uptown from downtown and the express from the local. Me, aboard the subway, I find myself hurtling toward Harlem when I want to get to Little Italy.

Q. John, you aren't trying. You're taking a disingenuous delight in this pose you have of being a hick. It excuses you from shouldering the discontents of civilization, from delivering, if I may say, the authentic depleted fin-de-siècle goods. Look at this so-called *Bech at Bay*. You really think I go about murdering people? You really think I could sleep with the Latina paralegal assistant of my attorney in Los Angeles when I was being sued by some quite implausibly loathsome talent agent? You think I go about jumping on women like that?

A. (*ominously*) People do.

Q. (*brushing past the obvious hot topic*) And this Jewishness you give me. What do you know about being Jewish? *Très peu*, I venture to estimate. As much as you learned listening to the *Jack Benny* program back in Shillington, Pennsylvania. Ask Cynthia Ozick. Ask Leon Wieseltier. Ask Orlando Cohen.

A. Cohen is my invention. Don't internalize your critics, Henry. It's death to the creative spirit. It breeds fictional tirades.

Q. You're no more Jewish than Henry Adams, and not near as funny about it.

A. It is my American right to give it a try, even in today's strident climate of defensive diversity. To be a writer at all, it seemed to me, is to be to some extent Jewish— outsiderish but chosen, condemned to live by your wits. Anyway, Henry, I don't see you as a Jewish writer. I see you as a Jewish writer, all but overwhelmed by the awesome possibilities of our trivialized profession. Like the whisky priest in *The Power and the Glory*—no matter how bad it gets, he can still put God in men's mouths. We can still put truth in men's heads. We share that, yes?—that boyish awe?

Q. I'll ask the questions, thanks. What I got out of your five tales, skimming through the galleys on the shuttle—a bumpy flight, by the way, especially over Providence— wasn't so much awe as terminal discouragement. If this is the literary life, give me *le silence éternel de ces espaces infinis* anytime.

A. It's true, the life isn't what it seemed in the tweedy days of Thornton Wilder and Bennett Cerf. And you reach an age when every sentence you write bumps into one you wrote thirty years ago. Each hard memory has only so many bits. Still, even into the shadows one must walk with faith. The enterprise has ever been thin, a mere dusting of words on the surface of the unsaid. That silence you mention always hangs on the other side of the paper. Still, in my limited experience, the barrel bottom remains moist, there has invariably been one more thing to say. Last summer, for me, you were it. I missed you. I missed New York. I had one leftover story, about

Czechoslovakia, that came too late for *Bech Is Back*, and wrote some to go with it, to make a book, a quasi-novel. You were my one more thing, and now, here we are, I am yours.

Q. (*grudgingly*) That's cute, I guess.

A. Excuse me, I must trim some bushes.

Despite Tough Guys, Life Is Not the Only School for Real Novelists

Kurt Vonnegut Jr.

The occasion for this piece was the publication by the University of Iowa Press of *A Community of Writers*, essays and recollections regarding the university's writers' workshop, collected and edited by Robert Dana, the poet and retired Cornell English professor. I taught full-time at the workshop in 1965 and 1966 and began writing my novel *Slaughterhouse-Five* while there.

I had gone broke, was out of print and had a lot of kids, so I needed the job most desperately. So did two other writers who took up temporary residence in Iowa City along with me, Nelson Algren and the Chilean José Donoso. I would later say of Paul Engle, who not only ran but personified and electrified the workshop for many decades, "The Coast Guard should give him a medal for all the drowning professional writers whose lives he's saved."

A year after I got there, Engle rescued an economically drowning Richard Yates, one of the most excellent writers I ever met, a second time. Engle, himself a poet, administered CPR in the form of a salary to poets, too: George Starbuck, John Berryman, Marvin Bell, James Tate, Robert Dana, Donald Justice and Robert Lowell, just to name a few.

And even though that was a third of a century ago, as I write, the names of students as well are fresh in my mind: Andre Dubus, Gail Godwin, Barry Jay Kaplan, Rick Boyer and John Irving and John Casey and David Nilob, again, just to name a few.

And Tennessee Williams and Flannery O'Connor long before my time. One wonders what ever became of them.

When the subject of creative writing courses is raised in company as sophisticated as readers of this paper, say, two virtually automatic responses can be expected. First a withering "Can you really teach anyone how to write?" An editor of this very paper asked me that only two days ago.

And then someone is almost certain to repeat a legend from the old days, when male American writers acted like tough guys, like Humphrey Bogart, to prove that they, although they were sensitive and liked beauty, were far from being homosexual. The Legend: A tough guy, I forget which one, is asked to speak to a creative writing class. He says: "What in hell are you doing here? Go home and glue your butts to a chair, and write and write until your heads fall off!" Or words to that effect.

My reply: "Listen, there were creative writing teachers long before there were creative writing courses, and they were called and continue to be called editors."

The *Times* guy who wondered if anybody could be taught how to write was taught how to write by editors. The tough guy who made students and their instructor feel like something the cat dragged in, possibly spitting on the floor after having done so, almost certainly, like me, handed in manuscripts to his publisher that were as much in need of repairs as what I got from the students at the workshop.

If the tough guy was Thomas Wolfe or Ernest Hemingway, he had the same creative writing teacher who suggested, on the basis of his long experience, how the writer might clean up the messes on paper that he had made. He was Maxwell Perkins, reputedly one of the greatest editors of fiction who ever lived.

So there you have it: A creative writing course provides experienced editors for inspired amateurs.

What could be simpler or more dignified? Or fun?

When I quit a good job at General Electric to become a freelance writer fifteen years earlier, there were only two degree-awarding graduate programs in creative writing in which short stories or poems or novels were accepted in lieu of theses: Iowa and Stanford.

I had attended neither one. To have done so would have been good for me. Vance Bourjaily, a permanent rather than transient member of the workshop faculty in my time, said he regretted not having apprenticed at Iowa or Stanford when he was starting out as a novelist. That would have saved him, he said, the several years he wasted trying to find out all by himself the best way to tell a story.

Much is known about how to tell a story, rules for sociability, for how to be a friend to a reader so the reader won't stop reading, how to be a good date on a blind date with a total stranger.

Some are more than two thousand years old, having been posited by Aristotle. I paraphrase Aristotle: If you want to be comical, write about people to whom the audience can feel superior; if you want to be tragical, write about at least one person to whom the audience is bound to feel inferior, and no fair having human problems solved by dumb luck or heavenly intervention.

And let me say at this point that the best creative writing teachers, like the best editors, excel at teaching, not necessarily at writing. While I taught at Iowa in the company of literary celebrities, the most helpful teachers there were two lesser-known writers named William Cotter Murray and Eugene Garber.

There are now at least a hundred creative writing programs in American colleges and universities, and even in Leipzig, Germany, as I would discover when I was there last October. That the subject is taught anywhere, given the daunting odds against anyone making a living writing stories or poems, might appear to be a scandal, as would be courses in pharmacy, if there were no such things as drugstores.

Yes, and our biggest secret about the Iowa Writers' Workshop was that it was one of the greatest teachers' colleges in the world.

The primary benefit of practicing any art, whether well or badly, is that it enables one's soul to grow. So the proliferation of creative writing courses is surely a good thing. Most came into being in response to demands by college students during the 1960s that their courses make more use of their natural impulses to be creative in ways that were not emphatically practical.

When I taught at Harvard for a year, for example, that was because students had asked for what they called "a creative track."

Chuffa, chuffa, chuffa. Choo choo. Woo woo.

When I taught at Iowa, then Harvard, then City College, here is what I tried to get away with, only in effect, not actually: I asked each student to open his or her mouth as wide as possible. I reached in with a thumb and forefinger to a point directly beneath his or her epiglottis. There is the free end of a spool of tape there.

I pinched it, then pulled it out gradually, gently, so as not to make the student gag. When I got several feet of it out where we could see it, the student and I read what was written there.

Metta to Muriel and Other Marvels: A Poet's Experience of Meditation

~

Alice Walker

At a recent weeklong silent retreat I had the insight that if I had not divorced my very admirable husband and suffered horribly the irrevocable loss of his friendship, I might never have discovered meditation. Although the ancient Chinese alerted us to the fact that one house move is equal to three fires, no one had told me how difficult it would be to separate from someone I loved deeply but did not wish to live with anymore.

I came to meditation, then, as most people do: out of intensity of pain. Loss, confusion, sadness. Anxiety attacks. Depression. Suicidal inclinations. Insomnia. A good friend told me about it, and I almost didn't listen because I knew she was having an affair with the teacher of meditation she so heartily endorsed. Still, the pain was unresponsive to everything else I tried.

I remember sitting on my cushion thinking this will never work, and then gradually, later in the night, realizing that I wasn't quite so jumpy, and that mornings no longer made me want to draw the covers over my head. I could listen to the radio, to music at least—which my soul had banned—almost normally, and in general it began to seem as if my inner vision had cleared.

After a week of lessons there was a ceremony announcing my mastery of technique. To my surprise at this event, during meditation, I felt myself drop into a completely different internal space. A space filled with the purest quiet, the most radiant peacefulness. I started to giggle and then to laugh. I knew I'd got it. And what I'd got was that meditation took me right back to my favorite place in childhood: gazing out into the landscape, merging with it and disappearing.

This is not what meditation is for everyone, of course. During a public dialogue with a master Buddhist teacher, Pema Chodron, I mentioned the joy of this "disappearing act." I said that it was probably what being dead would be like, and that you'd be surprised how much you enjoyed it. She said for her it was just the opposite. She felt, while meditating, totally present, aware of everything around her. Actually this has become more of what meditation is like for me as well, and though the Buddha teaches us not to cling, and especially not to cling to transitory states of consciousness, I do sometimes miss those brief moments of ego-absent bliss.

As I settled into meditation nearly twenty years ago, there in my two-and-a-half-room apartment, having given up the eleven-room house I'd lived in along with the admirable husband, I was surprised to find how many and how varied one's transitory states can be. There were sittings that were amazingly sexual, for instance, as if my *kundalini* energy had been waiting for me to sit down.

There were times when I wept copiously as old sorrows from the past put in their final bids for my undivided attention. There were times of pure joy, as I felt the lightness of heart that comes from knowing you've found something truly reliable and helpful.

Meditation has been a loyal friend to me. It has helped me write my books. I could not have written *Possessing the Secret of Joy* (about a woman who is genitally mutilated) without it; writing *The Temple of My Familiar* (my "great vision" novel of how the world got to be the way it is) would have been impossible. *The Color Purple* owes much of its humor and playfulness to the equanimity of my mind as I committed myself to a routine, daily practice.

It has helped me raise my child. Without it the challenge of being a single parent would have overcome me. It has made many losses bearable. Not just that of my former friend, the man I married, but the loss of other loved ones, communities, cultures, species, worlds in this time we live in, in which to honor our broken hearts, by peering quietly and regularly into the expanded opening, is to nurture a beginning to the re-creation of hope. And the magic of meditation remains.

It is a time when ancestors sometimes appear.

At the same silent retreat at which I understood how my early loss had led to a cherished gain, I became deeply engaged in *metta*, "loving kindness" meditation. We were being guided to send *metta* to a loved one, a benefactor, a neutral person and a difficult person. The difficult person is always rather amusing to choose, because the moment you do so, you begin to see how much that person resembles yourself.

But it was the benefactor that proved momentarily difficult. The *metta* that one sends is: "May you be happy. May you be safe. May you be peaceful. May you have ease of well being." The trouble was, I had so many benefactors to choose from.

I thought of two of my teachers, Howard Zinn and Staughton Lynd, historians and activists, who, while I was in college, taught me with the caring and patience of older brothers. I thought of Charles Merrill, a man who has made good use of the money his father (of Merrill Lynch) left him, by giving a lot of it away; some of it to me when I was a poor student, without even a pair of warm shoes. I thought of Marian Wright Edelman (of the Children's Defense Fund), whose work helping children benefits our whole society.

For a while all four of these people merged. But then just behind them rose the face of my poetry teacher, the woman I always said, behind her back of course, dressed like Henry VIII. Because she wore huge Russian-inspired hats made of fur, substantial boots and black-and-green clockwork tights. Muriel Rukeyser. Poet, rebel, visionary, life force.

It was the clearest I had been able to see her since I'd known her at Sarah Lawrence, and she looked nothing like she had—pale and weakened—in the years, much later, before she died. She looked ruddy and mirthful, and she was laughing. At Sarah Lawrence she had sent my very first poems to *The New Yorker* to be published. They were rejected; and just up from rural Georgia, I had no idea what *The New Yorker* was. But that she'd done it, instantly, on reading them, endeared her to me.

Later she would find an agent for me and introduce me to one of the great loves of my life, Langston Hughes. She would be the godmother to my first book of poems, as Hughes would be godfather to my first short story.

These two are prime examples of "the American race" I refer to in the dedication of my new book.

With much gratitude and emotion in my heart I began to send *metta* to Muriel.

May you be happy, I said.
I am happy, she said.
May you be safe, I said.
I am safe, she said.
May you be peaceful, I said.
I am peaceful, she said.
May you have ease of well-being, I said.
I have ease of well-being, she said.
May you be joyful, I added, just to be sure to cover
*   everything.*
I am joyful, she said. As if to say:
I'm in heaven, of course I'm joyful.

Heaven. Now there's a thought. Nothing has ever been able, ultimately, to convince me we live anywhere else. And that heaven, more a verb than a noun, more a condition than a place, is all about leading with the heart in whatever broken or ragged state it's in, stumbling forward in faith until, from time to time, we miraculously find our way. Our way to forgiveness, our way to letting go, our way to understanding, compassion and peace.

It is laughter, I think, that bubbles up at last and says, "Ho, I think we are there." And that *there* is always here.

In the Castle of Indolence
You Can Hear the Sound
of Your Own Mind

~

Paul West

Now and then my father would walk me down Market Street and Church Street to visit his mother's home, either to show me off like some chub or pike he had caught on one of his fishing expeditions or, more likely, to let me watch his four sisters and four brothers lying around reading books, oblivious of the workaday world but kept going by the beef sandwiches his mother plied them with all day. I was eight, perhaps, and they, he said, were shiftless.

Myself, I thought they were rather splendid, content to spend the day getting from one chapter to the next. (They read slowly, sometimes in a murmur.) They read adventure and romances, nothing heavy, though my father had read some Conrad and Dickens. But he, in his way, a one-eyed war veteran, was more imposing than they were, since every book was a continual out-of-focus effort. He preferred books he had read before. Coming from this print-hungry family, he had joined the Army to escape, and he now surveyed them all with his most sardonic military air: this was what he had been mutilated for, defending against the German hordes.

I linger on this ritual because later, in my undergraduate days, I discovered the Castle of Indolence and at once recognized it as 7 Church Row, where so long as you read, you were exempt from menial chores. From my father's siblings I gleaned the seeds of the contemplative life, the craving for a dream that shut the rest of the world out, the importance of the waterfall of images in my own head. Feeling at least as different from others as my father did with his wobbling gait and watery eye, I knew that lolling about and listening to my own mind, or to it in the act of engaging another's, I was creating the foundation for—what?

I wrote short stories about New Zealand fighter pilots who always survived against the Hun in the sun, as my model Cobber Cain had not. Those early stories have not survived either, but I recall installing in them, strangely enough, some echoes of my aunts' and uncles' literary indolence. The pilots felt at peace in the high altitudes, even when floating down by parachute after losing a dogfight. It was wartime after all, and a young nascent writer was bound to gather his dominant images from what, besides spent rounds, buzzed around him.

In a sense I had reproduced my father's margin of peace or ivory tower. Even while firing his Vickers machine gun or ducking shrapnel, he had calmed himself by murmuring the high-pitched orisons of monks heard I knew not where. (Gregorian chant, I guessed.)

It took me a long time, until my second novel, many years after my boyhood visits to Church Row, to realize that the indolence, the dream, the unconnectedness that seemed my heritage from my father's family, was the foundry where the novelist's work gets done, at least started; where unbidden *trouvailles* sprout up like pewits from a marsh, and structures lumber into view to support several chapters later on.

All I learned was that you had to give in to it, surrender even, reserving no moral or rational right to inspect the yield. I, who have always been able to sit for hours watching the sea or even the plains (from a high window in some Ramada), have managed to come up with grateful names for this fecund hinterland, most recently "the invisible riviera of the visible world."

It's not, some twenty novels later, quite a matter of switching on the spell, the tumult, the dream. I have to sit there at the keyboard and wait until the fantastic cavalcade of gorgeous brutes begins to come past my inward eye, and my evolution in their presence renews, my ransacking and extrapolating them begins. The blood pressure rises. The world disappears only to re-emerge from the kaleidoscope of tease. I feel lucky, on gentle terms with the Furies who goad me to be myself.

So the actual prose, a few phrases apart that simply swoop in, could not be more Apollonian, coldly designed; but what it evinces sometimes has a potent, mythic, even barbaric quality that makes me grope for such a word as anthropological. Quite recently, as I busied myself with what some would think an un-American activity, the novella, this one "about" Hitler as a failing/failed art student in Vienna, some renegade piece of my mind began intoning anti-Hitler doggerel over the rhythms and patterns of the main vehicle.

My novella attempts to explore the gentle impulse that led to gross, despotic violence and is serious, ironic, caustic stuff. The stanzas that came to mind were different, yet served no doubt as disdainful counterpoint. Perhaps Brecht would have understood this twitch of alienation effect:

> There was a young man from Vienna
> Who washed out his body with senna.
> He came out so thin,
> They sheathed him in tin,
> And now use him as an antenna.

The other bits of doggerel are different. All will make their way into the final text, worked in by a surreptitious hand. I base my decision on my feeling that the fable's manger is sometimes at least as interesting as the fable itself.

At the other extreme I have two-thirds done of a three-thousand-page novel conceived in defiance and written in joy. I have discussed this monster with only two people: an American publisher who without boning up can discourse on Hermann Broch's *Death of Virgil*, and my French publisher. The first blinked not and said only, "If you do it in paperback, the back will break." The second said: "Why not? Look at Proust. You do. *Eh bien*."

I write daily on a Smith Corona SL 580 from midnight to two, mostly to the sounds of classical music, no doubt a throwback to my mother's constant pianoforte cocooning me from the first, even in the womb. I respond best to piano music, so there must be something in my theory.

I had never realized that, say, 350 mornings times 3 pages approximates 1,000. It doesn't feel like much effort or much prose. If you have spent years delivering a weekly essay, as I did, this is more or less the way your mind works. I have always been able to sense the rhythm of the next five sentences and sometimes, so as not to lose it, chant it out in pseudo-language. If I felt like a freak as a child, imagine how much of a freak I feel now.

I should have heeded my mother and learned to play the piano, learned to read music. I suppose I have always felt an unpaid debt to her, a loving obeisance not made, in putting words in place of notes, to the woman who taught me grammar at her knee and indeed initiated me, for so long as I would listen, to the ingenuities of theory and harmony. I took what I needed from both sides of the family, never to complain. I am, by proxy, a product of the trenches and the Royal College of Music, vintage of Hubert Parry. I stay up long enough, usually, to correct what I've written, and on occasion to carve it up, then go to bed with that elated shiver of tasteful butchery well done.

If there is nowadays a backlash against fiction for not dealing with "the real world," such poppycock, then I deduce it's a backlash against imagination, which puts before the mind what was not there before. If we ever lose our awe before this complex emanation from the personality, then we will indeed be ready for the machine age, the hegemony of incessant data and dumbed-down reading.

But you can't just say the potent word *style* and leave it at that; it's just the key to not becoming anonymous. I know some writers who, maybe out of misplaced craving for uniformity (such as children like), want to write the same immigrant or primitive English. Perhaps they feel more noticeable because each has the heft of many clones. They aspire to an art of no mistakes, a low aspiration. The truth to this awkward dilemma must be existential, with the stylists surging up in the universe and thus defining themselves.

I once published an essay in defense of purple prose, since then much anthologized as a report from Cockaigne or Samarkand. In fact I was defending only the best purple, only the most lexically adroit style, reserving my fiercest applause for prose in which the simplest, most articulate combination of simple words most often appeared. Amid the abundance of the physical universe, it seems niggardly to write humdrum.

Of course the writer cannot always burn with a hard gemlike flame or a white heat, but it should be possible to be a chubby hot-water bottle, rendering maximum attentiveness in the most enterprising sentences. This is what I try for anyway, remembering I have learned self-assertion from Sartre, the enigma from De Quincey, from Beckett the performative erudite voice of the chronic emeritus, from Proust the art of never beginning, from Thomas Mann ironic solidity, and from Carlyle the luxuriant bouquet.

I have a porous vision, into which anything can get, and I welcome all invaders, knowing the world is richer by far than a wall of identical shoe boxes, whose mildewed aura defeats what's creative.

Why in earlier novels I have turned to historical figures—Jack the Ripper; Claus von Stauffenberg, who tried to kill Hitler with a briefcase bomb; Lord Byron's doctor; Klaus Barbie, and others—I can only say that ready-mades confer an enormous amount of creative freedom. Mixing real ghosts with imaginary ones thickens the total illusion and perhaps gives full vent to the notion that people "get to know celebrities." They get to guess or swallow propaganda, but that is all.

It is the mind that attracts us, whether of the serial killer, the dictator, the paragon or the flawed genius. When Elizabethan poets filched personages from myth, they called it "the matter of Greece and Rome." Ideal to pillage so as to have windup bathtub toys among us. The opera about Lizzie Borden has much the same effect.

These are incidentals, however. The novel form to which I have devoted so much time, and still attempt, is no mere story (favored word of newscasters), nor dialogue among scene settings, nor anything "well made," nor a page turner, so called, but a visionary plunge into what cannot be kept out of the mind, a "tale" its vehicle, that vision its tenor. If we have not yet learned this from Broch and Proust, Lowry and Frame, Joyce and Woolf, Lezama Lima and Roa Bastos, we have not learned much at all. Fiction is an attempt to control and accept the world, perhaps a reminder to all readers, and therefore on the side of life, that those who bite the bullet need not eat the gun.

A Sacred Magic Can Elevate the Secular Storyteller

Elie Wiesel

Most writers speak poorly about their work. And is *work* the right word? As a child I doubted that telling stories to strangers could be a serious endeavor, especially since often those stories were not even true. Everybody knows that stories are, by definition, the fantasies of those who don't know how to do anything else. I thought of writers as clumsy, lazy and frankly useless. Actually, one could very well live without them.

In the secular school I was sometimes forced to attend, my teachers made me read novels: first Romanian, then Hungarian novels. But I would lie if I said I remember their titles or the names of their authors, for I was too absorbed in my study of sacred literature. The stories and their commentaries about the binding of Isaac, Jacob's fight with the angel, the Revelation at Sinai or Moses' solitary death interested me much more than the fictional adventures of our national writers.

And then there was the Talmud with its often stormy

debates, the spellbinding power of Midrashic legends. I loved to plunge into their deep waters. There were times, as I tried to solve ancient questions with the help of masters and disciples of long ago, that I would smile, responding to the magic of personal encounters.

Still, the Hasidic stories were my favorite. To hear my maternal grandfather tell them in his nostalgic yet lively manner was to be transported into a world apart, a vivid realm in which the wicked always ended humbled and punished, whereas their victims forgot their misfortunes and found themselves invoking their right to happiness. In short, this was a world in which miracles were part of everyday life.

Of all the Hasidic tales, the ones I loved best were those told by Franz Kafka's predecessor, the celebrated and mysterious Rabbi Nahman of Bratslav. They made me dream. When Kafka, the great novelist from Prague, spoke of his wish to see his tales turned into prayers, he was more than likely thinking of Rabbi Nahman. Only he did the reverse: he transformed his prayers into tales. Was Rabbi Nahman then Kafka's teacher? Perhaps, but surely he is mine.

I still feel close to his beggars and madmen roaming through forests inhabited by princes in love with exiled princesses. There one hears the wondrous songs that lift the soul to its celestial roots but also the harsh laughter that signals the nefarious presence of demons ready to tear apart the heart of man so as to consolidate their eternal reign.

I confess that had I not been drawn to that strange and beautiful universe, I might not have written some of my books, surely not those that reflect my love for the Hasidic tradition.

But what about my other books, my novels? Or my short stories, essays and plays?

My very first book, *Night*, was, paradoxically, born more in certainty than doubt. I knew I had to testify about my past but did not know how to go about it. Here, neither Talmudic sages nor Rabbi Nahman and his peers were of much help. In fact, in spite of all my readings—for in the meantime I had studied French, German and American classics—I felt incapable and perhaps unworthy of fulfilling my task as survivor and messenger. I had things to say but not the words to say them.

Acutely aware of the poverty of my means, language became obstacle. At every page I thought, "That's not it." So I began again with other verbs and other images. No, that wasn't it either. But what exactly was that "it" I was searching for? It must have been all that eludes us, hidden behind a veil so as not to be stolen, usurped and trivialized. Words seemed weak and pale.

Which ones could be used to tell of the long journey in sealed cattle cars toward the unknown? And of the discovery of a twisted and cold universe where some people came to kill and others to die? And of the separation, during nights engulfed by flames, the brutal disruption of families, what words could describe them? And the disappearance of a small Jewish child so wise and so beautiful when she smiled, killed together with her mother the very night of their arrival? Before these images, all words disintegrate and fall lifeless into the ashes.

And yet it was necessary to continue. And speak without words; more precisely, without the proper words. And to try to trust the silence that surrounds and transcends them, while knowing, "That was still not it."

Is this the reason why the manuscript—written in Yiddish, my mother tongue, and translated first into French and

260

then into English—was rejected by all the major publishers in France and the United States? In New York a renowned editor justified her rejection in a letter to my literary agent: "Anyway, this author will never write another book."

She was right on one point: I never wrote another book about my wartime experiences. *Night* silenced in me the voices that clamored to be heard. Anyway, I thought, people will not listen.

To a friend who wanted to know why I tend to avoid the subject of Auschwitz in my work, I answered, "Woe to the writer who is overwhelmed by his subject." Instead I chose to write on the Bible, the Talmud and Hasidism, and novels on Jerusalem, the Middle Ages, mysticism, Communism and Alzheimer's disease, all so as not to find myself among the dead. There were moments when I regretted the times when, faithful to my vow, I let silence be my only link to the violent but mute world of my nightmares.

Miraculously, my first small volume got a good reception. Was it the writing, or was I protected by the event it described? Reviewers seemed to like me. Perhaps they agreed with the skeptical New York editor who felt I would never write another book: Why "kill" him since he is already half dead?

I considered myself lucky. And I was. My second book was also a succès d'estime. Yet a voice inside me kept warning me by whispering Napoleon's mother's wise comment "If it would only last." Well, it did not. The next book brought me my first negative review. Why deny it? I was miserable. I wanted to go from newsstand to newsstand and buy up every single copy of the daily containing the unkind evaluation of my novel. Later I learned to cope with nastiness better than with praise.

Now with the passing of years I know that the fate of books is not unlike that of human beings: some bring joy, others anguish. Yet one must resist the urge to throw away pen and paper. After all, authentic writers write even if there is little chance for them to be published; they write because they cannot do otherwise, like Kafka's messenger who is privy to a terrible and imperious truth that no one is willing to receive but is nonetheless compelled to go on.

Were he to stop, to choose another road, his life would become banal and sterile. Writers write because they cannot allow the characters that inhabit them to suffocate them. These characters want to get out, to breathe fresh air and partake of the wine of friendship; were they to remain locked in, they would forcibly break down the walls. It is they who force the writer to tell their stories.

Writing, however, is getting more and more difficult. Not to repeat oneself is every writer's obsession. Not to slide into sentimentality, not to imitate, not to spread oneself too thin. To respect words that are heavy with their own past. Every word both separates and links; it depends on the writer whether it becomes wound or balm, curse or promise. It would be simple and comfortable to play with words and win; all it takes is to play the game and practice a bit of self-delusion.

But for my generation, playing games is not an option. We need to bear witness, we need to hope, with Rabbi Nahman of Bratslav, that with a measure of luck, some of our testimonies will safeguard the essence of our prayer.

Ultimately the Jewish boy from my little Jewish town was wrong: writing is anything but easy.

Embarking Together on Solitary Journeys

~

Hilma Wolitzer

The proliferation of writers' workshops in his country raises that old question: Can creative writing be taught? The best answer I've ever heard is Wallace Stegner's two-parter: "1. It can be done. 2. It can't be done to everybody."

I suppose he meant that only genuine talent can be nurtured and developed in the right atmosphere. But in my experience just a handful of workshop students ever exhibit such talent, and we all know of gifted writers who work well without the benefit of organized groups or individual mentors. It must also be said that talent can be inhibited, if not destroyed, under the wrong circumstances. So do we actually need all those workshops?

Writing fiction is a solitary occupation but not really a lonely one. The writer's head is mobbed with characters, images and language, making the creative process something like eavesdropping at a party for which you've had the fun of drawing up the guest list. Loneliness usually doesn't set in until the work is finished, and all the partygoers and their imagined universe have disappeared.

Doubt tends to creep in then, too. Is this story finished? Is it any good? How can I tell? Most writers' hearts are divided by ambition and self-doubt. Even Virginia Woolf pondered, about her manuscript of *To the Lighthouse*, "Is it nonsense, is it brilliance?" Of course she might have asked one of her famous Bloomsbury bunch for an informed opinion.

But most neophytes aren't so well connected, and seeking help with your work from nonwriter spouses and friends can be disastrous. People who love you tend to love whatever you produce because it's yours. (Didn't your mother proudly display your early artistic efforts on her refrigerator?) And those with hidden agendas of competitiveness or downright envy might try to sabotage your confidence and your burgeoning career.

Remember Gore Vidal's candidly mean-spirited observation: "Whenever a friend succeeds a little, something in me dies." And my grandmother's: "With friends like that, you don't need enemies."

Bringing one's work home, so to speak, can be very bad for personal relationships. Another member of your household may be put into the untenable position of live-in critic, and watch out: he may be planning to show you something he's written, counting on reciprocal love. A fairly safe comment in those circumstances is: "This is terrific, sweetheart. I couldn't put it down." How would anybody dare to put it down with you standing right there, wringing your hands and silently moving your lips during the reading?

You must ask yourself if you really want an honest opinion from a loved one. The soon-to-be ex-wife of a popular novelist once complained about his habit of asking her to read a chapter of his work in progress at bedtime.

"If I say I like it," she said, sighing, "he wants to know how much, and, in minute detail, exactly why. And if I don't like it, he's so disappointed I have to cheer him up. In either case we don't get to sleep for hours."

She had my sympathy, but so did he. When I recount last night's dream for my psychologist husband at breakfast, I secretly want him to admire it, not analyze it.

I remember completing a draft of my first short story and wondering if it worked, if it was, in fact, a bona fide story. Reading it over and over again didn't resolve my uncertainty. I desperately needed some feedback, but I didn't have a community of peers to turn to; I didn't know any other writers at all.

I was a typical '60s housewife then, deeply involved in the minutiae of daily household life. Most of my creative energy was spent in homemaking. I never made a simple tuna salad sandwich for my children. Those poor kids got to cannibalize tuna fish men with carrot-stick limbs and bulging olive eyes. Birthday cakes—made from scratch of course—were decorated to the point of collapse, and my Jell-O molds were famous for their originality and complexity.

As a late-blooming writer I'm sometimes asked if my husband and children felt abandoned or betrayed by my sudden new career. Frankly, I think the whole family was relieved when I began to direct all my energy and inspiration elsewhere. Still, I didn't know where that first story came from (although the opening line, "Today a woman went mad in the supermarket," might have given me a clue) or what in the world to do with it.

So I asked my husband what he thought, and wisely he suggested I seek professional advice, which led to my taking a writing workshop at the New School. There, for the first time, I found the company of other writers. Stanley couldn't have been any happier to have found Livingstone. But my joy wasn't immediate.

The workshop I joined was led by Anatole Broyard, a writer who would later become a daily book reviewer for the *New York Times*. I'd submitted a short story, as required, and several days later received a card inviting me to show up at a designated classroom at 6 P.M. on the following Monday.

The room was packed that first evening (hadn't they turned anyone down?), and I sat in one of the few available seats in the back, wondering what I was doing there and why it had seemed like such a terrific idea when my husband suggested it. Anatole made a few opening remarks and then, after consulting a list, called on me to come up front and read my story aloud to the class. Caught off guard, I had to spit out my gum and stumble forward, dropping a few pages along the way. I was so nervous I almost hyperventilated, and I read with the dramatic expression usually reserved for the laundry list or the eye chart.

When Anatole asked the class to respond to my story, a man in the back promptly pronounced it the most boring thing he'd ever heard. That was about all I cared to hear. I was ready to pack it in, to go home and just make Jell-O molds and tuna fish men for the rest of my life.

Anatole slipped me a note, even as he told my detractor that he had every right to dislike my story, but that he had to say why he had found it boring and what I might do to make it better. And wasn't there anything in it he had liked? The last thing I wanted at that moment was detailed negative criticism, or even being thrown a belated bone of praise, but I half-listened anyway, as I surreptitiously opened the note, which I still have and still look at occasionally for reassurance. It said: "The story is fine. Congratulations. See me later."

Those words tempered the sting of the harsh ones my classmate was still blithely offering, and in that moment I learned the most important thing about teaching writing: There must be a balance of honesty and charity in the workshop. Everyone must be aware of a fellow human being behind the work being discussed, and criticism has to be useful, not just derogatory or laudatory.

When I spoke to Anatole after class that first, fateful night, he suggested that I join his advanced workshop, a much smaller group that met weekly in a conference room at the advertising agency where he worked during the day. I was so relieved and flattered. I went home with buoyed self-confidence, and the following week I read the same story aloud again, with a lot more expression this time, not to mention much higher expectations.

To my disappointment several members of the advanced group didn't like it much either. But at least their comments were balanced and constructive, and I was able to listen more calmly and extract what I needed to improve the story.

I learned a lot of other things over the years I stayed in that group: that the workshop isn't group therapy; that character prevails in fiction just as it does in life; that the common workshop goal is revision, not suicide; that work should never be submitted anonymously (unless you're in the federal witness protection program); and that there's really no defense of a manuscript that doesn't work for the reader. Best of all, I gradually came to realize that I'd joined a staunch fellowship of writers who would support me through difficult projects, spells of writer's block, and those inevitable rejections.

I've taught fiction writing on and off for a number of years now myself, and those basic principles of honesty and charity are still at the core of my workshops, just as the company of other writers continues to sustain and inspire me and my students. Every story presented gets a fair shake, even (and this once really happened) when it's told from the point of view of a brain-dead person. Credibility and empathy, as you can imagine, were big issues during that session.

I still agree with Wallace Stegner that talent is a prerequisite for the future professional. But there's a place in the classroom for other interested parties who, in their ardent analysis of one another's writing, become much better readers. And God knows we can always use more of them.